VICTORY IN NORMANDY

By the same author

*

All in the Day's March
(Autobiography)

VICTORY IN NORMANDY

By

Major-General David Belchem

Head of Field-Marshal Montgomery's Operations and Planning Staff,
1943–45

1981
Chatto & Windus
London

Published by
Chatto & Windus Ltd.
40 William IV Street
London WC2N 4DF

Editor: Martyn Bramwell
Design: Mel Petersen & Associates
Designer: Nigel O'Gorman
Cartographer: Tom Stalker-Miller
Picture Research: John McClancy

© Russel Sharp Ltd. 1981

Text set by Tameside Filmsetting Ltd.
Ashton-under-Lyne, Lancashire

Designed and produced by
Russel Sharp Limited
9 Queen Street
Horsham, West Sussex RH13 5AA

Printed and bound in Hong Kong by
Dai Nippon Printing Co. (HK) Ltd.

British Library Cataloguing in Publication Data
Belchem, David
    Victory in Normandy.
    1. World War, 1939–1945 – Campaigns – France –
    Normandy
    I. Title
    940.54'21   DA756.5.N6
    ISBN 0-7011-2546-2

Contents

7   **PREFACE**
Major-General David Belchem CB,
CBE, DSO

8–25   **PART I**
OBJECTIVE NORMANDY
Re-entry into Western Europe, 1944:
Origins of the Allied Plan
The Choice of the Assault Area

26–39   **PART II**
THE ATLANTIC WALL
The German Forces in France

40–71   **PART III**
**THE PLANNING OF
'OVERLORD'**
The Allied Plan of Campaign
Operation 'Bodyguard': The Deception
Plan
The Preparatory Operations
The Detailed Plan of Assault

72–121   **PART IV**
THE D-DAY ASSAULT
The Airborne Landings
The Seaborne Assault
Reflections at the end of D-Day

122–145   **PART V**
**THE ALLIED
BRIDGEHEAD**
Establishment of the Bridgehead:
7–12 June
Development of the Bridgehead:
13–19 June
The Capture of Cherbourg and the
Establishment of the Odon Bridgehead
The Great Set-back

146–175   **PART VI**
THE BREAK-OUT
Preparations for Operation 'Cobra'
Break-out on the Western Flank
The Encirclement

176–183   **PART VII**
**PERSPECTIVE ON
NORMANDY**
A Review of the Battle

184–187   **APPENDIX**
The Battlefield Cemeteries and
Memorials

188–191   **INDEX**
191   **GLOSSARY**
192   **BIBLIOGRAPHY**
192   **ACKNOWLEDGEMENTS**

Preface

The battle for Normandy, fought between the beginning of
June and the end of August, 1944, will remain a subject of
great interest for many years to come – not only to
historians and to future generations of the armed forces,
but also to the descendants of the men who fought there:
men from Britain, America and Canada; from France,
Germany and Austria; and from the Netherlands, Norway,
Poland and a number of other countries.

Because Normandy is an area blessed with excellent
beaches backed by a delightful rural countryside, and also a
province with a unique historical and religious heritage –
from the great tapestry at Bayeux, celebrating William the
Conqueror's invasion of Britain in 1066, to the impressive
Basilica of Sainte Thérèse at Lisieux – it has naturally
become a centre for tourists from many parts of the world,
many of whom visit the great battlefields of the last war
just as visitors to Belgium visit the historic field of
Waterloo.

My object here is to present in a concise narrative, the
preparation, planning and execution of the battle for
Normandy and, where possible, to answer some of the
questions that have for many years clouded the central
issues.

Before becoming involved in the Normandy campaign I
experienced at first hand the calamitous intervention in
Greece and Crete in 1941, and during the North Africa
campaign I served on the staffs of Generals Wavell,
Cunningham, Ritchie and Auchinleck. I joined Field-
Marshal Montgomery's staff when he arrived in the desert
in August 1942. After the battle of El Alamein I returned to
regimental duty as Brigade Major of 2 Armoured Brigade,
and thereafter commanded 1 Royal Tank Regiment.

At the end of the campaign in North Africa I returned to Montgomery's staff, first as a Lieutenant-Colonel in the Operations staff and later, on promotion, became head of the Operations and Planning Staff – a position I was to hold until the end of the war. Consequently I was closely involved at all stages of the planning and execution of the invasion plan and the subsequent operations inland, and on many occasions acted as Montgomery's Chief-of-Staff when General de Guingand was absent from the front.

This account is based largely on notes I made at the time these historic events were taking place, and from several months of exacting, and rewarding, work immediately after the Armistice when I drafted, under Montgomery's direction, the original (military) editions of his formal accounts, *Alamein to the Sangro* and *Normandy to the Baltic*.

I would like to express my thanks to Dr Noble Frankland, Director of the Imperial War Museum, and to Mr James Lucas of the Museum's Photographic Department, and Mr R. Simkins of the Research Department, for their expert help: and to my editor Martyn Bramwell and his colleagues at Russel Sharp Limited for their skilful presentation of the book, and particularly its excellent maps and diagrams.

The secretarial services of Mrs Padmore and Mrs Quayle of Rottingdean are gratefully appreciated.

David Belchem.

David Belchem
Hove, Sussex
December 1980

Objective
Normandy

RE-ENTRY INTO WESTERN EUROPE, 1944:
ORIGIN OF THE ALLIED PLAN

In December 1941, following the surprise Japanese attack on the US Pacific Fleet in Pearl Habor, Hawaii, President Roosevelt and Prime Minister Churchill agreed to unify the war effort of their two countries. By April 1942, in spite of the many differences that subsequently arose about the strategy to be adopted for defeating Hitler's Reich, it was agreed that when the required resources became available the ultimate aim would be to launch a mighty assault from England to breach the coastal defences of 'Fortress Europe' and thrust deep into the heart of Germany.

Back in 1942, Churchill had organized a British Combined Services Committee and charged it with the task of studying the subject, and at the Casablanca conference in January 1943 the two leaders, with their combined Chiefs of Staff, agreed to set up an Anglo-American Inter-Service Headquarters in readiness for the time when a Supreme Commander would be appointed to finalize plans for the invasion of Western Europe. Lieut.-General F. E. Morgan was made Chief of Staff to the Supreme Allied Commander (designate). His title was shortened to COSSAC, and he was given an American Deputy, Brig.-General R. W. Barker.

Serious planning began at once, and immediately revealed the magnitude of the problem and above all the immense quantity and diversity of resources which would be needed to ensure success. These included many major facilities and items of equipment that had yet to be conceived, or which at best were only in a preliminary stage of technical development.

In brief, after a series of conferences, Roosevelt and Churchill agreed on 6 December, 1943, that the Supreme Commander should be an American – General Eisenhower. The announcement was made at the end of the month and the organization of the staffs began

Dwight D. Eisenhower
General Eisenhower, in command of the Western Task Force, photographed a few days before sending his troops into French Morocco on 5 October 1942. Fourteen months later he was appointed Supreme Commander of the Allied Expeditionary Force for the assault on northwest Europe.

Pearl Harbor
The devastating attack on the U.S. Pacific Fleet in Pearl Harbor, Hawaii, in 1941, precipitated the immediate commitment of America's armed forces.

SHAEF commanders
*Reading from the left are:
Lt. Gen. Omar Bradley,
Senior Commander, American
Ground Forces; Admiral Sir
Bertram Ramsey, Allied
Naval Commander; Air Chief
Marshal Sir Arthur Tedder,
Deputy Supreme Commander;
General Eisenhower, Supreme
Commander; General Sir
Bernard Montgomery, C-in-C
British Army Group; Air
Chief Marshal Sir Trafford
Leigh-Mallory, Air C-in-C;
and Lt.Gen. Beddel Smith,
Chief-of-Staff, SHAEF.
The Allied commanders
were supported by a well-
knit headquarters staff,
the main elements of which
are represented on the
lines-of-command diagram
on the facing page.*

immediately. At Eisenhower's Supreme HQ Allied Expeditionary Force (SHAEF), Air Chief Marshal Sir Arthur Tedder was appointed Deputy Supreme Commander, with Lieut.-General (US) Bedell-Smith as Chief of Staff. The Allied Naval HQ and Allied Air Forces HQ for the invasion forces were placed, respectively, under Admiral Sir Bertram Ramsay RN, and Air Chief Marshal Sir Trafford Leigh-Mallory RAF. No corresponding Commander-in-Chief was appointed for the land forces, but Eisenhower delegated to General Montgomery the overall command of the British and American forces for the initial phase. Montgomery was made directly responsible to Eisenhower for planning and implementing the seaborne assault, and for the subsequent operations on the Continent until such time that numerically the strength of American forces engaged in the battle exceeded that of the Commonwealth (British and Canadian) forces. At that point, Eisenhower would himself take over direct command of all the armies and Montgomery would revert to the command of 21 British Army Group (which initially comprised fourteen British and two Canadian divisions). It was assumed, on the basis of the planned build-up of Allied invasion forces, that this hand-over to Eisenhower would take place ninety days after D-Day.

On 31 December, 1943, Montgomery, having relinquished command of the Eighth Army in Italy, arrived in Marrakesh, Morocco, for a meeting with Churchill, who was convalescing there after a bout of pneumonia, and Eisenhower, who was *en route* to the United States. Churchill had a copy of the COSSAC plan with him, which he showed to Montgomery. After studying it, Montgomery declared that it was not viable, and Eisenhower – who had already seen it – agreed. The strength and distribution of forces proposed by COSSAC for an invasion in the Baie de la Seine were insufficient to ensure success.

Montgomery went on to London, to start rethinking the plan in conjunction with Ramsay and Leigh-Mallory. The COSSAC staff was disbanded, and its members were redistributed among the newly organized staffs of SHAEF and the individual armed services headquarters. General Morgan was among the senior officers transferred to the new SHAEF staff.

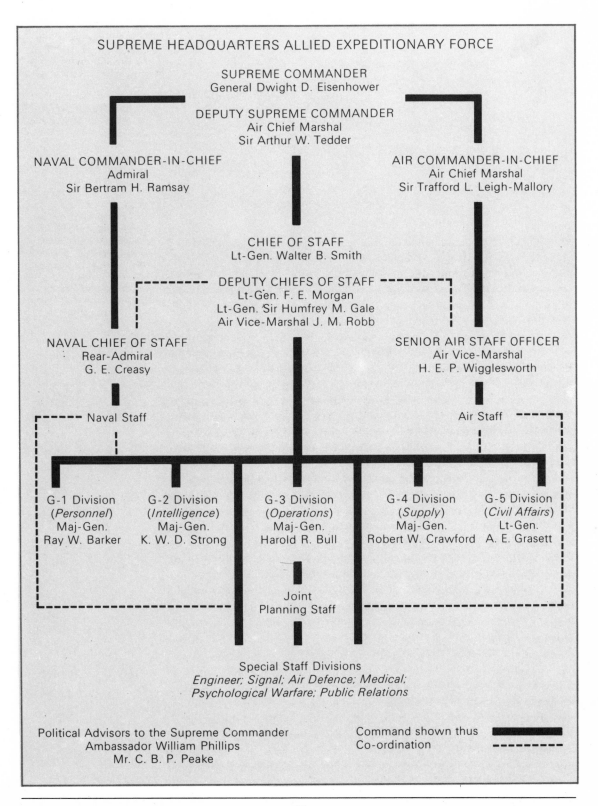

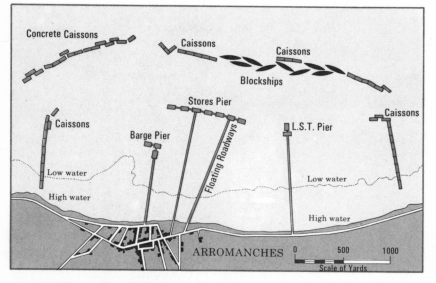

More than two million tons of prefabricated steel and concrete were to be towed across the Channel to form the two artificial harbours.

The Mulberry Concept

The proposed Allied landing on the west coast of Europe, and the subsequent penetration inland, involved planning the greatest sea-borne assault in the history of warfare, against the strongest coast defence system ever devised. For the planning staffs, who had to complete their task by the beginning of June when the assault operation was to be launched, an immense amount of detailed work lay ahead. Fortunately the three service Commanders-in-Chief were able to make arrangements for most of the senior members of the inter-service planning teams that had worked together on the invasion of Sicily and Italy to be brought back to Britain for OVERLORD – the codename adopted for the invasion of Normandy. This proved a great advantage as we already knew and had confidence in one another. Moreover, we had all gained invaluable experience in the techniques required, and the problems to be expected, in the mounting of an invasion operation involving all three services.

Although the COSSAC operational plan had been discarded, because it was based on inadequate resources and because Montgomery disagreed with its strategic concept, the work COSSAC had done in conjunction with the Combined Operations HQ (under Admiral Mountbatten and other service departments) proved invaluable. This was especially true of certain longer term projects, which required considerable time and effort to conceive, design and construct, and which Montgomery's planning staff, together with the other service staffs, could not have been able to realize in the limited time available before D-Day. One of the most crucial of these projects was the design and building of two artificial harbours, the components of which would have to be towed from Britain across the Channel to the invasion assault area.

Floating caissons
More than 200 massive preformed concrete caissons, some the size of five-storey buildings, were built in Britain for the D-Day assault on Normandy.

One of the basic assumptions was that any port captured by the invasion forces would be mined; its quays, cranes and handling equipment damaged or destroyed by the retreating German forces. Indeed, the British had already had some experience of this at Tripoli and at Sousse. Somehow, provision had to be made for an area of sheltered water offshore, from which men, equipment and stores could be safely unloaded from ships and carried to the beach. Churchill himself put forward the idea of floating piers for direct ship-to-shore unloading. As long ago as World War I, when at the Admiralty, he had suggested the possibility of designing a concrete breakwater and he revived this idea in 1942 when the problems of open-beach unloading came under close examination. In a note to Admiral Mountbatten dated 30 May, 1942, Churchill again stressed the need to develop the concept of breakwaters and floating piers – ending his note with the now-famous words, 'Do not argue the matter. The difficulties will argue for themselves.'

In June 1943, the need to design and prepare two artificial harbours was agreed by all concerned, but by the time the preliminary plans had been considered, only some eight or nine months remained for the technical design and development work to be undertaken, and for the production of an immense quantity of components and equipment to be completed.

The two prefabricated harbours, codenamed 'Mulberries', were an extension of the outer breakwater system designed to provide an area of sheltered water at each of the five assault beaches designated in Montgomery's final plan. Each beach was to be protected by an offshore breakwater, or 'Gooseberry', formed by a number of old ships ('Corncobs') steamed into position and then sunk in line parallel to the shore. Hollow ferro-concrete caissons, towed into position and sunk, would fill any gaps in the blockship line.

On two of the beaches, OMAHA in the American sector, and GOLD in the British sector, the Gooseberry breakwaters were to be enlarged to form artificial harbours. Flanking breakwaters, again formed by lines of ferro-concrete caissons, would extend the Gooseberry shorewards and enclose an area about the size of Dover harbour. Inside each Mulberry would be three floating piers against which barges, shallow-draught vessels and vehicle-landing ships could off-load in relatively calm water. Floating roadways, towed into position in sections and there bolted together, completed the artificial harbour facilities by linking the piers to the beach. Areas of deeper water within the protection of the Gooseberry breakwater were designated as mooring stations for deeper draught vessels.

In all, some two million tons of preformed steel and concrete had to be towed or carried by sea to form the two Mulberries, including more than 200 caissons, some of them the size of five-storey buildings, and 70 block-ships. All available tugs in Britain, and even some from America, were requisitioned for the massive towing operation.

The wide variety of special equipment that had to be designed and produced for OVERLORD also included a flexible pipeline to carry vehicle fuel across the Channel. Made of special aluminium alloy, the pipeline could be wound on massive reels fixed to the sterns of cable-laying ships to be paid out and then sunk on the sea bed. From a pumping station in southeast England, vehicle fuel could then be sent under pressure to a filling station on the Continent or to a relay pumping station to extend the pipeline inland. This project, called PLUTO (Pipe Line Under The Ocean), was to prove a great success: by September 1944 the overland extension was supplying vehicle fuel to Allied troops deep inside Belgium.

Production facilities had also to be found in Britain and America for a wide range of specialized landing craft and assault vehicles. These included ships designed to carry personnel; artillery pieces that could fire during the run-in to the shore; rocket-firing mattresses, and tanks – including engineer assault tanks for demolishing thick concrete obstacles, flail tanks for clearing paths through minefields, carpet-laying tanks to cover clay patches revealed below high tide, flame-thrower tanks and bridge-forming tanks. The special armoured tracked vehicles also included another innovation – amphibious (DD) tanks intended to accompany the leading waves of infantry as they stormed the beaches.

The need for such design, technical development and industrial production tasks had been foreseen and to some extent initiated by COSSAC, but it still took time for the people involved to grasp the sheer size of the task that lay ahead. For instance, when the Anglo-American allies first decided that their major aim would be to force an entry into Western Europe from Britain, General Marshall, Chief of Staff of the US Army, advised Roosevelt that the target date should be in 1943; he even suggested that if the situation in Russia were to become desperate, an emergency operation might be neces-

Mulberry section
One of the more complex sections of the Arromanche 'Mulberry' undergoing its final tests before moving to its holding area.

sary in 1942. But as they studied the situation, and gained more experience of the operational requirements of a major invasion operation, General Marshall and his US colleagues came to agree with the British view that the earliest possible date for OVERLORD would have to be in 1944. Marshall appreciated that, apart from the industrial bottlenecks that were bound to occur, certain essential preliminary requirements had to be fulfilled before a seaborne invasion could be launched. In addition, he realized that preparatory operational tasks, combined with an increasingly complex Deception Plan, would be needed to pave the way for the assault, once the target area had been decided. Another most important factor was that in 1942 and the early part of 1943, priority in ship construction and repair had to be given to the needs of the Allied navies if they were to win the critical Battle of the Atlantic, and this in turn meant cutting down production of landing craft, many of which were also required by US forces fighting in the Pacific against the Japanese.

For all these reasons the date for Operation OVERLORD had, short of some wholly unexpected collapse of the German Army, to be delayed until 1944. To have attempted to break into the European continental coast defences prematurely would have invited disaster, as the raid made by the Canadian Army on Dieppe in August 1942 had already shown.

Prerequisites to OVERLORD

Before they could hope to mount a successful invasion from Britain, the Allies had to achieve two interim goals. In the simplest terms, they had to win the Battle of the Atlantic, and establish complete mastery over the German air force (Luftwaffe) in Western Europe.

It was essential that within reasonable bounds the freedom of passage of troops, equipment and stores of all kinds between the North American continent and the United Kingdom was assured, and despite the appalling losses of shipping in 1942, and in the early part of 1943, the Allied navies had achieved this situation by mid-1943. 'ULTRA', the system by which German wireless messages were intercepted and decoded in the UK, played an important part in the Atlantic battle, particularly when it became possible to determine the location of the ships that carried fuel and supplies for the German U-boat packs. With this detailed intelligence the Royal Navy and RAF Coastal Command were able to attack the submarines

at their re-supply points, or when approaching them.

Equally vital to the success of the invasion plan was the need to deny the Luftwaffe any opportunity of harrassing the massive fleet which would be involved in the initial assault and in the follow-up operations. On D-Day alone, by a marvel of organization, several thousand vessels of all types were to be manoeuvred through mine-swept channels to the assault area, and within a few days up to 7,000 seaborne units of all categories were destined to become involved in transit, at ports and terminals in Britain, or at the landing beaches. As the operations developed farther inland, the maintenance of air cover would assume an ever increasing dimension.

The subjugation of the Luftwaffe involved complex strategical and tactical offensives, including bombing attacks on German oil refineries and stocks and on aircraft factories and airfields. By early 1944 the Allied air forces had achieved mastery in the air over Western Europe, and with the sea lanes of the Atlantic also secured, conditions were ripe for the preparatory stages of OVERLORD.

The war at sea *(left)*
The entry splash of a perfectly placed depth charge marks the end of a German submarine in the closing stages of the Battle of the Atlantic. The line of machine-gun fire from the Sunderland's rear turret straddled the enemy vessel, killing its captain and coxswain.

Airfield attack
A Republic P-47 fighter of US 8th Air Force makes a close attacking run on a flak tower guarding an airfield in northern France. The P-47 was developed to give cover to the long-range bombers of the US Air Force. It had far greater operational range than the Spitfire and was one of the most important aircraft used in the battle for air supremacy.

Spitfire sortie
Operational range was a major factor in deploying British and American air force resources. Spitfires and Hurricanes were used against coastal targets, for reconnaisance, and for virtually all night-fighter operations, while the longer-range American aircraft took on targets further inland.

THE CHOICE OF THE ASSAULT AREA

Operation OVERLORD, as defined at the beginning of January 1944 in Churchill's directive to the Combined Chiefs of Staff, was *'to mount and carry out an operation with forces and equipment established in the UK and with target date 1 May, 1944, to secure a lodgment on the Continent from which further offensive operations could be developed. . . .'*

Before examining the enemy's dispositions, the planners' first task was to decide upon the most suitable area or areas for landing on the Continent, bearing in mind the particular needs of the three services.

The air forces' requirements proved to be the chief limiting factor. To provide the necessary air cover over the sea lanes from Britain, roughly half the fighter aircraft used had to be Spitfires of the RAF which, having a relatively restricted operational range, had to be based initially at airfields in Britain. Extensive use of naval aircraft carriers was impractical. Quite apart from the fact that the war in the Pacific took priority in the allocation of carriers, the number that would have been required to service an invasion force for a relatively long period in Europe was beyond Allied resources. Moreover, when working at intensive rates, seaborne aircraft of that period still had to make frequent returns to a land base because repair and overhaul facilities on board the carriers were very limited.

A Spitfire based in southeastern England had only sufficient fuel to cross the Channel, locate and attack a target and return to base,

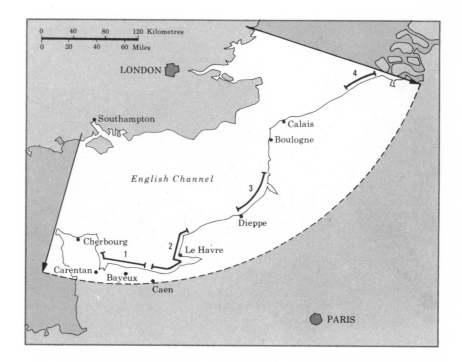

on a frontage from Flushing in southern Holland to the Cherbourg (Cotentin) Peninsula. Thus the choice of entry to the Continent had to be within these set limits.

Naval requirements imposed the next most important constraint. Even in summer the weather in the English Channel can be very bad, with prolonged gales and high seas moving in from the Atlantic. The only sector within the invasion limits which offered some degree of shelter in such conditions was to leeward of the Cherbourg Peninsula, in the Baie de la Seine: the Navy therefore opted for the Normandy coast.

Army requirements were straightforward. As far as possible, troops had to be landed on beaches relatively free from clay patches at low tide and with direct access to flat and reasonably open terrain where tanks, guns and vehicles could be rapidly deployed for the advance inland.

The air force required the army to capture hinterland terrain that was flat and open (such as farm land) where airstrips could readily be bulldozed. Initially these would be used for quick refuelling, though some would later be developed into 'permanent' air bases. In the pre-jet era, propeller-driven aircraft could land and take off from airstrips covered with heavy metal mesh sheets anchored to the ground.

Given these various limiting factors, the Allied choice was restricted to four areas: southern Holland–Belgium, the Somme estuary, the Seine estuary, and Normandy.

The Low Countries were not acceptable because the hinterland is

Coastal battery
Key areas of the French coast were defended by huge naval guns. When firing to sea, these guns came under the command of Admiral Kranke but when fire was directed on the beaches they came under command of the army. Such complications in command structure were to prove a serious weakness in the German defensive operation.

criss-crossed by literally hundreds of canals and waterways, many of which constitute major obstacles to cross-country movement. Advancing troops would inevitably suffer delays, and be vulnerable to counter-attack, as bottlenecks developed at the bridge points. The Somme was not suitable because the river precluded an advance on a wide frontage. No army can operate efficiently astride a major water line because it restricts the ability to switch resources between the divided flanks, unless numerous crossings are established. That in turn means landing heavy bridging equipment in the very early stages of the assault when the essential requirement is for fighting units with their weaponry. The Seine estuary was ruled out because of the known density of heavy coastal defence artillery around Le Havre (and the same applied to Cherbourg). The Allied navies could not risk the heavy losses that would have been incurred had ships and craft come within range of those ports.

There remained the sector of coastline between the eastern coast of the Cherbourg Peninsula and the River Orne. At the time planning started in January 1944, we knew from RAF reconnaissance photographs that the German 'Atlantic Wall' defences on this part of the coast were markedly less well developed than elsewhere within the boundaries available to us. Also, the beaches along this stretch of coast were suitable for troop landings, with the exception of one sector between Arromanches-les-Bains and the River Vire where there were a number of submerged offshore rock outcrops, and also some cliffs with steep bluffs near to the shore. However, even this difficult section offered one stretch of four miles within which a landing beach could be established. There were also some rocky outcrops in the sea to the north-northeast of Caen, but they did not constitute a continuous obstacle to the passage of landing craft.

Underwater traps
This photograph, taken at the lowest point of the tide, shows the vast array of obstacles, many of them fitted with explosive charges, protecting a typical stretch of coast.

Otherwise the conditions for landing troops and vehicles were propitious. Although the transit distance from southern British ports was on average about 100 miles, Normandy offered two important advantages for which there were no equivalents elsewhere. First, it lay within relatively close reach of the Brittany ports and sheltered bays – and we had to assume that Cherbourg itself would be too heavily damaged to be of much use for some time. Second, in the long run, Normandy provided access to a most appropriate Lodgment Area or Development Zone; that is, a large area inland from the invasion beaches which could be cordoned off using the minimum defence forces. Normally, once invasion troops are firmly established ashore, a time arrives when the initial momentum of the assault begins to flag. Leading formations require reorganization and if possible a 'breather' while repairing equipment and absorbing replacements, and fresh divisions must be landed in order to build up the concentration of forces in the Deployment Zone in readiness for resumption of the offensive. Ports have to be cleared and the air forces need to establish airstrips (and eventually bases) to increase the operational range of their aircraft. Stocks have to be built up for future operations and meanwhile the overall commander must finalize his forward plan, having made his appreciation of the enemy situation and of his own strategic policy, tactical planning and logistical capabilities.

So far as landing in Normandy was concerned, the major rivers Seine and Loire formed a most appropriate natural boundary for a Deployment Zone. The defeated German Army – its defeat had to be assumed, otherwise the operation could not have been viable – would be forced to withdraw behind these water lines in an attempt to limit the invasion to the northwest part of France. In such an

Bocage country
A German Panzer rumbles into position along one of the narrow high-banked lanes typical of bocage country. In many areas the lanes were so narrow, and the banks so steep, that tanks, lorries and other large vehicles were quite unable to turn round.

event the Allied forces could face the enemy across these river obstacles while needing only a minimal force to cover their own reorganization. In order to deal with the gap between the Seine and Loire, to the southeast of Chartres, an airborne formation could be dropped to complete the Allied cordon.

The possibility of a brief pause in the Deployment Zone also meant that Montgomery would be able to hand over direct operational control to Eisenhower in an efficient manner, and the SHAEF staff would have at least a little time in which to assume the responsibility of serving Eisenhower in the day-to-day direction of operations.

Despite the advantages enumerated, there remained one major disadvantage in landing in Normandy. The hinterland, though mostly flat, is *bocage* country. The word is difficult to translate, but broadly it means mixed woodland and pasture terrain, with numerous winding side-roads and lanes bounded on both sides by high levees or banks topped by tall, thick hedgerows which greatly limit visibility. The *bocage* is therefore much more suitable for defensive infantry action than for an offensive operation requiring fast and effective deployment of armoured divisions. In addition to this, parts of the Carentan estuary and the area lying to the west of it are crossed by hundreds of minor water courses running through swampy ground, while the villages and farms of northwestern France are built of heavy stone slabs, providing perfect cover from small-arms fire.

Worse still, only the area to the south and southeast of Caen is suitable for scraping airstrips quickly, which is why the air forces favoured the Somme estuary sector, bounded to the east by rolling open farmland. However, after careful study of the needs of all the Allied services, and taking account of the German appreciation of where the Allies were most *likely* to land. Normandy was decided upon – unanimously at the planning stage, although it was later to cause serious misgivings to the leaders of the tactical air forces.

The terrain problem
These two pictures clearly illustrate the contrast in terrain which was at the heart of the conflict between Tedder and Montgomery during the formative phase of development of the plan for the invasion. The photograph right shows typical bocage while that below shows the open farmland, ideal for airstrip construction, found in the area around Falaise. To Tedder, the early establishment of forward airfields was of paramount importance.

PART II

The Atlantic Wall

Beach defences: 1944
Three lines of massive steel obstacles bedded in concrete protect this gently sloping beach in northern France. A temporary railway line has been laid to facilitate the movement of heavy materials but the use of horses illustrates German concern over the shortages of vehicle fuel caused by Allied bombing.

THE GERMAN FORCES IN FRANCE

By the month of June 1944, the German order of battle in France comprised four armies under Field-Marshal Von Rundstedt, amounting to some 58 divisions – about one-fifth of Hitler's field army. They were organized into two army groups. 'B' Group, which Field-Marshal Rommel (previously the Allies' opponent in Tunisia) took over in February, had the Seventh Army covering Normandy and Brittany with 16 divisions, and the Fifteenth Army of 25 divisions covering the Channel coast from the Seine valley to Holland. 'G' Group, under General Blaskowitz, comprised the First and Nineteenth Armies, totalling 17 divisions, stationed on the Biscay and Riviera coasts respectively. The German forces included nine Panzer (armoured) divisions, and one Panzer Grenadier division consisting mainly of mobile infantry in armoured half-tracks. The calibre of the divisions varied from the highest order of Panzer and field infantry formations to second-line static coast-defence troops, which included conscripted Poles and reluctant nationals of other central European countries.

The defences of the 'Atlantic Wall' had been developing for several years. First priority had been given to the main port areas, which by 1944 had become virtually impregnable to seaborne assault. Next came the Pas de Calais at the Channel straits, which the Germans considered the most likely area for an Allied invasion attempt. But elsewhere the defences were less formidable. The Baie de la Seine coast had a system of linear defences based on a string of strongpoints manned mainly by coastal defence troops.

The gun emplacements were of concrete and armour protected by extensive minefields, wire entanglements and a great variety of obstacles including walls insurmountable by tanks. In addition, extensive areas of low-lying terrain had been deliberately flooded by breaching the dykes, particularly in the marshy country around the Carentan estuary. On the beaches themselves, and extending over varying distances below high-water mark, there were underwater obstacles of various kinds designed to halt and impale landing craft,

The waiting game
German infantrymen, manning a heavy machine-gun emplacement, look out across the English Channel in 1942. At this time the first steps were being taken to seal the coast of France against any Allied attempt to regain entry into Europe.

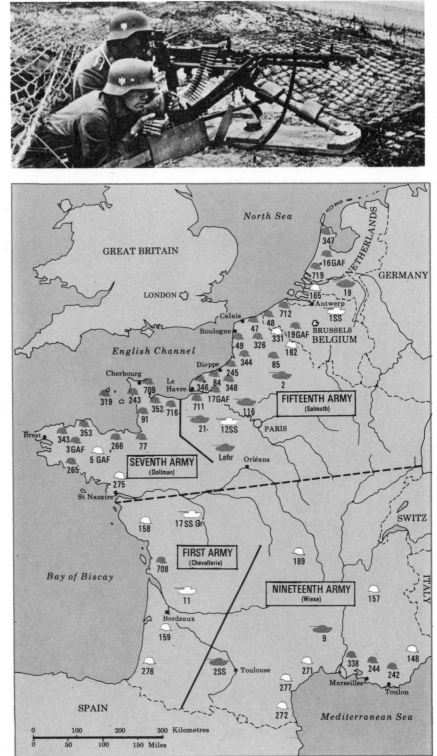

German dispositions in France

– – – – – Army Group Boundary

———— Army Boundary

 Infantry Division

GAF Division

Panzer Division

Refitting or forming

By June 1944, German troop strength in northern France represented almost one-fifth of Hitler's total field army.

North Sea

GREAT BRITAIN

NETHERLANDS

GERMANY

347

16GAF

719

165   19

Antwerp

LONDON

712

1SS

Calais   47   48

Boulogne   326   331   19GAF

49   182   BRUSSELS

BELGIUM

English Channel   344

Dieppe   245   85

Cherbourg   84   2

Le Havre   346   348

709   711   FIFTEENTH ARMY

319   243   17GAF   (Salmuth)

352   716   116

91   21   12SS   PARIS

Brest   353

343   266   77

3GAF   Lehr   Orléans

5 GAF   265   SEVENTH ARMY

(Dollman)

275

St Nazaire

158   17 SS Gr

SWITZ

FIRST ARMY   189

(Chevallerie)

708   ITALY

Bay of Biscay   NINETEENTH ARMY

11   (Wiese)   157

Bordeaux

159   9

148

276   2SS   Toulouse   271   338   244   242

Marseilles

277   Toulon

SPAIN   272   Mediterranean Sea

0   100   200   300 Kilometres

0   50   100   150 Miles

and to cripple them by explosive charges attached to poles and triggered by impact. Many of the coastal artillery emplacements were sited well forward, and behind them, to a depth of up to three or four miles, were field and medium artillery batteries well placed to engage approaching craft and bring fire to bear on any enemy troops who might succeed in landing on the shore.

When we had started planning in January, the Normandy coast defences had not been as well developed as those elsewhere, but when Rommel took over, the Germans immediately stepped up the installation of obstacles, particularly of the underwater type. Rommel also ordered anti-landing devices to be placed on potential dropping and landing areas and as these indications reached us by analysis of aerial photography, they naturally caused some anxiety.

The German Atlantic Wall was a formidable barrier and the air

Teller mine (*above*)
To conserve steel for the war effort, many of the beach obstacles were built of wood and in addition to forming a physical barrier many were also armed with Teller mines (land mines), artillery shells, or improvised charges. The posts were angled seawards to impale incoming craft and the explosives were armed with impact detonators.

Coastal battery (*left*)
Heavy batteries, encased in massive concrete might withstand a direct hit but they proved vulnerable to a near miss as any distortion of the battery foundations would render the sophisticated radar-controlled gun-laying equipment useless.

reconnaissance photographs of the underwater obstacles and fortifications along the shore appeared forbidding indeed. Only in retrospect were we to learn that the German commanders were conscious of the shortcomings of the Wall. Von Rundstedt, the Commander-in-Chief, West, was obliged at Hitler's insistence to be prepared for an Allied assault in *any* sector of the coast from Holland to the south of France, including even the coast of Spain and Portugal. Leaving out the Iberian Peninsula, the German problem was to cover a coast of some 4,800 kilometres with a force of 58 divisions, the majority of which were second-line static defence troops. The linear density was thus less than one division per 80 kilometres. Even with modern weaponry, the classic defence scale is of the order of one first-line division deployed in depth per ten kilometres.

Final preparations: 1944
Knowing that an invasion was imminent, and conscious of weaknesses in the Atlantic Wall, Field-Marshal Rommel ordered a rapid acceleration of the defensive programme in the early part of 1944. Leaving nothing to chance he made frequent personal visits to inspect the installations.

The 'Atlantic Wall' (right)
The huge guns guarding key ports and estuaries were on permanent alert and seconds only were required to strip away the camouflage curtains and bring the guns to bear on any approaching enemy.

Conflict in the High Command

Von Rundstedt and Rommel were both convinced that the Atlantic Wall defences should be fully manned in depth on the stretches of coast most likely to be selected by the Allies for their assault. Elsewhere, only a thinly held screen could be provided. But it appears that after the Anglo-American landings in Morocco and Algeria in 1942, and the fall of Tunis in May 1943, Hitler became increasingly apprehensive about the possibility of an Allied offensive in the south of France combined with a pincer invasion in the Bay of Biscay. It is curious that there appeared to be no general appreciation, on the German side at this period, of the power and importance of air forces in the conduct of land warfare, particularly as far as the *tactical* air forces were concerned. Only after the war were some surviving German officers recorded as saying that they considered the idea of an Allied landing in the Bay of Biscay irrelevant because the region was beyond the range of tactical air support by forces based in Britain.

The rapid acceleration of work on the Normandy coastal defences after Rommel took command of Army Group 'B' in February 1944, and the constant flow of intelligence from agents in Europe and from ULTRA intercepts, made it very clear to the Allied planners that there was a conflict within the German High Command. Rommel's military skill, and his experience of action against the Allies in northern Africa, led him to disagree fundamentally with the disposition of the German Panzer reserves adopted by Von Rundstedt and Schweppenburg. (The latter was in charge of Panzer Group West, responsible for the training and administration of the armoured divisions in France and, in the event of an Allied invasion, for their command in battle.)

At the heart of this conflict of opinion lay the tactical methods to be adopted in the event of an Allied invasion of Europe. Rommel's preferred tactics were to repulse the enemy while they were actually landing on the beaches – and this philosophy certainly matched British military thinking. As the invading troops are wading ashore, loaded with weapons and equipment and probably cold, wet and suffering from seasickness as well, they are vulnerable to attack. It takes some time for them to get sorted out and form up into a disciplined and co-ordinated assault array. Hence Rommel's strengthening of the beach defences; his siting of artillery so as to give maximum concentration of fire-power on to the landing areas, and his insistence that the Panzer formations should be sited well forward, poised to strike hard and fast at the attackers. From his desert war experience Rommel well knew the devastating effect that tactical air strikes could have on ground troops, and fully appreciated that any attempts to bring up Panzer divisions from deep positions would be frustrated and delayed by incessant air attack by the virtually unopposed Allied air forces.

Inspection *(right)*
Field-Marshal Rommel
and Lt.-Gen. Hans
Speidel checking progress
on the Atlantic Wall.

Von Rundstedt
Initially, Field-Marshal
Von Rundstedt was in
charge of coastal defence
of the 'West Wall' from
Holland to southern
France, but his relation-
ship with Hitler was a
difficult one and on at
least two occasions he
was replaced by other
commanders – only to be
reinstated again later.

Von Rundstedt, on the other hand, believed in the 'crust-cushion-hammer' concept, in which a 'crust' of static defenders, manning the coastline, would determine the geographical limits of an Allied attack, which would then be contained by a strong 'cushion' of infantry formations close in the rear. Held farther back in strategic reserve would be the 'hammer' – the armoured divisions, which would launch decisive counter-attacks through the cordon and throw the invader back into the sea.

Hitler was certainly impressed by the arguments of his favourite general but was also swayed by Schweppenburg, who visited him in an attempt to persuade him that the armoured divisions should be held under a centralized control in the forested areas astride the Seine. The result was an unsatisfactory compromise of the six Panzer divisions in Army Group 'B': three were to remain as a strategic reserve under the control of OKW, Hitler's personal HQ; the other three would be allocated to Von Rundstedt's command, subject to OKW approval of any proposed movement or commitment. Von Rundstedt was thus left with insufficient means to mount quickly a major counter-attack on any Allied landing, and equally unable to concentrate his resources for a rapid counter-offensive against an established Allied bridgehead.

In 1943, the German High Command was fed with a series of spurious agents' reports and rumours about the Allies' preparations for an invasion in Western Europe. The Allied deception planners were largely responsible for the rumours which reached the Germans from several foreign diplomatic sources, including embassies, which had been deliberately 'misinformed'. At this early stage, Hitler became increasingly anxious about the wide variety of areas which he thought the Allies might choose for an assault, including

21 Panzer *(left)*
Elements of 21 Panzer Division move into new positions in a village south of Caen having been transferred from Brittany in May 1944.

Von Rundstedt
Field-Marshal Carl von Rundstedt arrives for a senior staff meeting in northern France

northern Italy, the south of France, Spain, Portugal, the Bay of Biscay, Brittany, Normandy, the Pas de Calais, Holland, Denmark and Norway. Thus the Führer imposed upon his generals an un-co-ordinated compromise defence policy.

Further 'ULTRA' intercepts revealed that Von Rundstedt was so conscious of the inadequacy of the resources available to him in France and the Low Countries that he made a desperate appeal to Hitler that the German forces south of the Loire should be withdrawn to northern and central France. This would have created a strong reserve for the 'hammer' force, which Von Rundstedt's defence policy demanded, of three Panzer divisions, four first-line and four second-line infantry divisions (excluding five training divisions). But Hitler would not listen to such ideas; his standard instruction to his generals was that they should look to their own front, and that OKW would take care of everything else.

By early 1944 it was clear from intelligence reports and from direct observation, that Hitler had decided that the Allied attack would be launched in the Pas de Calais sector. Rommel certainly expected an attack in the Baie de la Seine, between Caen and the Cherbourg Peninsula, and there were strong indications that he also anticipated a second invasion in the sector astride the River Somme directed southwards towards Le Havre, but we had no indication of whether he anticipated that the Normandy landings would constitute the Allies' *schwerpunkt* (the focal point of the main assault) or a diversionary operation to assist the more northerly attack.

Only after the war were we able to confirm our suspicions that

The V1 threat
Although crude by modern standards, Hitler's V1 'Flying Bomb' presented a major threat to London and to Allied morale. The launching sites for these weapons were to become a major target for Allied operations, and pressure to end the V1 assault on London may have contributed to the decision to launch the ill-fated airborne attack at Arnhem.

Von Rundstedt believed the main Allied effort would be made in the Pas de Calais. His reasoning was that the Straits of Dover presented the shortest sea crossing and that, if successful, the landings would create a bridgehead only four days' march by armoured forces from the Ruhr. In addition to these considerations, he took into account the forthcoming start of the V1 flying bomb offensive against London, knowing that the launching sites would be in the Pas de Calais region. The German generals had all been assured that the V-bombs would bring Britain to her knees. As far as Normandy was concerned, the general view seemed to be that any landing in the area would have as its purpose the capture of Cherbourg.

Nevertheless, Hitler was, it appears, influenced by Rommel's anxiety about Normandy. On 6 May he signalled to Von Rundstedt that he attached great importance to Cherbourg and the Normandy coast, and ordered all possible measures to be taken to reinforce the area. As a result, 91 Division was sent to the Cherbourg Peninsula together with a parachute regiment; 21 Panzer Division was moved from Brittany to a location south of Caen, and Panzer Lehr Division, the strongest armoured division in the German Army, was brought from Hungary and sited south of Chartres.

These reinforcements significantly increased the forces south of the Seine, but they did not indicate that Hitler had changed his mind about the Pas de Calais priority. While he regarded 12SS Panzer, 21 Panzer, and Panzer Lehr divisions as the reserve covering the Seventh Army sector, the other three armoured divisions north of the Seine remained directly under his control.

Manning the wall
Reinforcements arrive at the coast as part of Rommel's continuing efforts to strengthen the more vulnerable sections of the Atlantic Wall.

As far as I know, there is no authenticated explanation of why Hitler finally rejected Rommel's urgent pleas concerning this very vital matter, but the extent to which the Führer was influenced by the Allied deception plans must have been a major factor.

The only personal account I can offer comes from a discussion I had in 1971 with General Kaltenbrunner, who had been Chief of Staff to Admiral Canaris, Hitler's Chief of Intelligence. I asked him why Hitler had discarded the possibility of the main assault being delivered in Normandy, since for purely professional reasons the choice was a likely one, to say the least. Moreover, intelligence reports of high rating which Hitler received from 'Cicero' – a German spy working in the British Embassy in Ankara, Turkey – had indicated Normandy. Kaltenbrunner's reply was that Hitler had, by the month of May, received such a mountain of conflicting reports about where and when the invasion would take place, that he finally threw the lot at Canaris, stating that the only reliable source was his own intuition, backed by a favourable horoscope, and that on that basis he believed the Allies' *schwerpunkt* would certainly come in the Pas de Calais area.

Cicero's information was in fact photographed from genuine Foreign Office documents, but it appears that it was largely discredited. This may well have been the result of the deception achieved by the seemingly official documents planted on the Germans by the stratagem of 'the man who never was', a body washed up on the Spanish shore from a British submarine in 1943. These documents reached Berlin from the German Ambassador in Madrid, who was later dismissed when the documents proved to be a fake.

Attempts to provide Hitler with reliable intelligence information were, from March 1944, made increasingly difficult. Admiral Canaris had been discharged, and his Foreign Intelligence Service wound up. Intelligence became part of Hitler's Central Security Office, headed by General Kaltenbrunner and inefficient as Canaris's operation had been (and the Admiral himself was anti-Nazi), the changed system proved even less effective.

Ready for action
German infantry, armed with machine guns and grenades, burst from the entrance to their dug-out position in a full-scale practice alert.

The Allied Assessment

It is important at this point to consider the level of enemy resistance which the Allied planners anticipated would be concentrated against the Normandy landings. In the invasion sector between Caen and the southeastern part of the Cherbourg Peninsula, it was anticipated that on D-Day the German garrison would amount to three coast defence divisions (243, 709 and 716); two first-line infantry divisions (91 and 352), and one Panzer formation, 21.

The rate of enemy build-up against our assault was difficult indeed to predict. So much depended on the influence of the Deception Plan, which was designed to indicate that the main Allied effort would be made in the Pas de Calais. Equally the degree to which the air interdiction programme and the tactical air force operations, together with French Resistance sabotage, would delay the movement of enemy reserves towards the combat area, could not be precisely calculated, although we could at least assume that no bridges would be left intact over the Seine west of Paris, nor over the Loire as far east as Orleans.

It was assumed that as a result of the airborne divisions arriving during the night of D—1/D, and the extent of the seaborne assault on D-Day, the enemy would realize that OVERLORD was a major operation (diversionary or otherwise), and that the nearest available armoured and mobile infantry reserves would be summoned to oppose the Allied incursion and to deliver immediate counter-attacks down to the beaches. When these proved unavailing, it was presumed that the enemy would concentrate his reserve forces and deliver heavy co-ordinated counter-attacks in selected areas, particularly in the sectors of Caen and Carentan. Such counter-attacks were expected to develop about D+4 or D+5, by which time it was estimated that he would have some six Panzer divisions available.

By D+6 the Allies expected to be facing a total German force of twenty divisions, including eight Panzer formations, and it was anticipated that by D+8, or at the latest by D+12, the Germans would adopt a policy of cordoning our bridgehead to prevent further Allied advances inland. For this, logically, they would bring infantry divisions to the front in order to relieve the Panzers, which would be concentrated for an all-out counter-stroke.

When studying the battle later it will be seen that because of the shortage of infantry, Panzer divisions had to be utilized to plug holes in the German defence lines. As a result, the élite armoured troops were worn down in a static role when it was to be expected that they would have been replaced by infantry and re-formed in readiness for a massive counter-attack.

That many of the anticipated developments did not materialize, or were attempted only very much later, greatly assisted the Allies, and our original assessment of German reactions to the invasion, made in January and February, was happily modified during April and May. It had been thought that Hitler would be able to transfer up to fifteen divisions into Western Europe from other fronts, but the mounting successes of the Soviet forces on the eastern front, and the Allied progress in Italy, rendered such transfers increasingly unlikely. By the beginning of June, Kesselring's forces in Italy were in full retreat, while in Russia the Germans had been driven out of the Crimea and were facing a major Soviet offensive.

The German naval forces in the west consisted of a few destroyers and torpedo vessels, together with a number of motor torpedo boats and patrol craft. The naval commander was also responsible for the heavy coastal artillery batteries, which were equipped with radar. In theory, when the guns were firing to seaward they came under naval control, whereas fire directed on the beaches was controlled by the army. The Luftwaffe in France had a total force of about 890 aircraft of all categories, from bombers, fighters and night fighters to reconnaissance and transport squadrons, but such was the Allied mastery in the air that this arm of the German fighting machine was impotent. But perhaps the greatest weakness in the Atlantic Wall lay in its command structure. There was no centralized control of the three German services on the western front: each service had its own chain of command back to Berlin. As a result, swift co-ordinated action against an enemy incursion was virtually impossible: indeed, there was no single high authority on the spot to direct such action and the resultant muddled operational command system greatly weakened the power and speed of the German reaction when the invasion started.

In the period immediately before D-Day, the Luftwaffe carried out very little air reconnaissance. On 5 June, only five German aircraft made routine sorties over the English Channel, and although the Allied 'armada' was by then on the move, the planes returned to base with 'nothing to report'. On the same day, German naval patrols in the Channel were cancelled because of bad weather. Such were the German weather reports that Rommel himself was already on his way to southern Germany to visit his family.

Channel observers
A mobile observer crew equipped with a powerful telescope, scans the Channel from a vantage point near Calaise. From this area the most powerful of the German army's guns were able to direct fire on Dover.

A spent force

Well before the planned date for the invasion of Normandy, the German Air Force had ceased to present a serious threat. Allied air supremacy was complete, and total control of the skies over northern France was to prove a major factor in the success of the landings.

The turning point

More than 240,000 tons of Allied shipping was sunk during the first half of 1943. But by the end of the year the tide had turned: the cracking of the German ULTRA code, and the capture, intact, of a German U-boat code book, enabled the Allies to attack the marauding submarines when most vulnerable – when forced to surface and rendezvous with their supply ships. Within months, Allied losses had virtually ceased: the sealanes between Britain and the United States were secure, and preparations for the invasion could proceed.

PART III

The Planning of 'Overlord'

THE ALLIED PLAN OF CAMPAIGN

The first phase of planning for Operation OVERLORD concerned the assault itself and the initial objectives for the leading wave and follow-up forces when they began their penetration inland. Since the detailed planning of all three services had to be related to the Army's strategic and tactical plan, Montgomery had to produce his proposals quickly, once he arrived back in England on 2 January, 1944. He began by formulating his views on the measures required to convert the COSSAC plan into a practical proposition, and then started discussions with Admiral Ramsay and Air Chief Marshal Leigh-Mallory to obtain their reactions.

While accepting the Baie de la Seine as the invasion sector, Montgomery proposed that the frontage of assault should be increased to 50 miles, extending westwards from the River Orne to include a landing beach on the southeastern coast of the Cherbourg Peninsula. The wider frontage would then include forces poised for the rapid capture of the port of Cherbourg. It would involve five distinct divisional assault areas, which would be divided into separate sectors for First US and Second British Armies, thus affording separate logistical supply routings.

The American sector

UTAH   Assault areas

UNCLE   Landing beaches

US Airborne Division

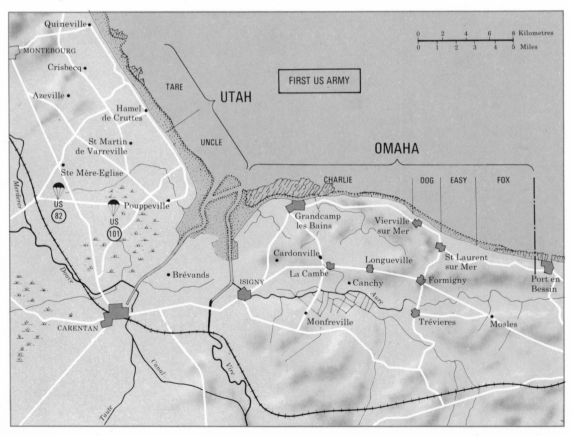

First US Army would be allocated the *western* sector comprising two assault areas: the first from about Quinéville, on the eastern coast of the Cherbourg Peninsula to the River Vire, and the second from the River Vire up to, but excluding, the town of Port-en-Bessin. Second British Army front in the *eastern* sector would extend from Port-en-Bessin to the River Orne. Three assault areas would be located in this sector: the landing beaches will be defined later.

The location of the US sector on the west flank would, in time, be convenient for direct shipment of reinforcements and stores from America to Cherbourg and the Brittany ports, while the British sector was well sited for transit of supplies from southern England.

Each of the five landing beaches was made the responsibility of a Corps Commander, with his HQ staff. Each beach was designated specific objectives and each had its own independent logistical supply lines. We had learnt in the Mediterranean to avoid the passage of a division from one Corps through an assault area established by a different Corps. It could all too easily lead to delays in deployment and it required duplication of communications.

Ramsay and Leigh-Mallory agreed to this outline, which was approved by Eisenhower on 21 January, when he returned from the United States. It should be added that the Admiral still had mis-

The British sector

GOLD   Assault areas

ITEM   Landing beaches

Brit   British Airborne Division

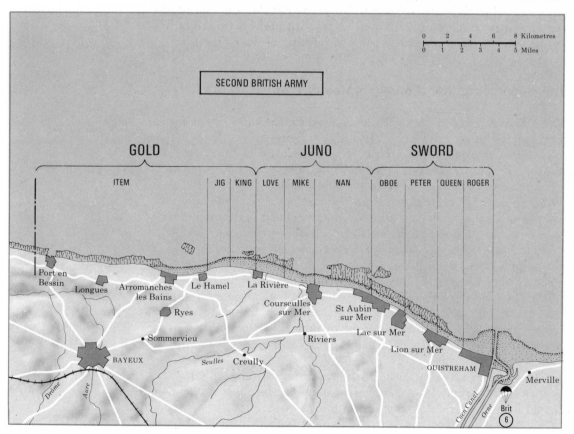

Assault training
A major problem facing the invasion planners was the shortage of time available for training the crews of the vessels involved, and the thousands of men destined to cross the beaches. Long stretches of the British coastline were closed to all but military personnel and in the months before D-Day were used for intensive training. Photographs, left and facing, show American infantry undergoing their final assault practice.

givings about the target date of 31 May, not on account of the plan, but because of the time required for the training of the crews who were to man the landing craft. However, the Combined Chiefs of Staff agreed to the date, subject to the study of tidal and moonlight conditions in the first week in June. A moonlit night was mandatory for the manoeuvres of naval craft, aircraft and airborne troops.

Development of Montgomery's Master Plan

The manner in which the plan was evolved for the subsequent battle of Normandy up to the line of the Rivers Seine and Loire must be considered in some detail. This is one of the most controversial subjects of the period and, as head of Montgomery's planning staff, I am anxious to record the facts as I knew them.

There has been much speculation about *when* the master plan for operations up to the River Seine was made: indeed even the fact that it was made in London *before D-Day* has been challenged. This question can readily be resolved. But it has also been declared that the original master plan was altered or modified during the course of operations between D-Day and the time that the Allies closed up to the River Seine. This was not the case, but I well understand how certain timings and important events which occurred during the battle led to misunderstandings even among responsible senior officers – American and British – and, more recently, among competent historians.

Montgomery was concerned with the strategy to be adopted by the Allied armies from the coastal assault up to the Seine, where he would hand over direct command to Eisenhower.

The first phase required the establishment of a firm beach-head at

each of the five landing beaches. Each beach-head would extend, initially, for about one mile along the coastline, and then be enlarged to a depth inland of up to six or even eight miles. In this process, the immediate requirement was to push the enemy back far enough to deny him observation over the landing beaches so that he could not direct fire on specific targets of craft and troops there, nor determine exactly what was coming ashore. Thereafter, the penetration inland depended on the first objectives to be reached, which might be a strategic town or village, an important road axis, or a dominating feature on the ground which had to be seized from the enemy. Once the first objectives had been gained, the first-phase advance was to proceed farther – if our troops had still the stamina to overcome whatever resistance the enemy presented.

This definition of a beach-head is based on the assumed (planning) forecast of what it was hoped to achieve on D-Day, and was therefore subject to a number of imponderables, most important of which were the strength and competence of the enemy defences; the influence of the weather on air operations and other means of fire support; the state of training and leadership, and the physical limitations of the soldiers.

The concurrent requirement in the beach-head was to reach outwards from the flanks in order to link up with adjacent beach-heads. This involved clearing the enemy from the gaps between the landing beaches. Ideally this operation should have been accomplished on D-Day, but whether it would prove possible was open to some doubt, particularly in the case of the interval between UTAH and OMAHA, where the water obstacles, and flooding in the Carentan estuary region, were so extensive.

The beaches had to be linked up into one continuous bridgehead as quickly as possible, and the bridgehead in turn extended inland, so that the Allies had a firm base from which to operate. The other priority task was to capture the port of Cherbourg as a first step towards relieving the Mulberry harbours, however long it might take to get the port installations working and the waters cleared of mines. This requirement was obviously going to involve a tricky operation for First US Army, because it amounted to clearing the whole peninsula of enemy, and stretching a cordon of troops across the base from the Carentan area to the western shore to prevent enemy reinforcements being sent to Cherbourg. The cordon would, of course, be facing south. At the same time, First Army would be sending forces northwards to surround and capture the port. Only when that had been done could the whole Army be concentrated in the south, all facing the same way.

Until the whole of First US Army was facing in the same direction, its cordon in the south could not be expected to have the strength to launch any major offensive southwards. It followed that the forces

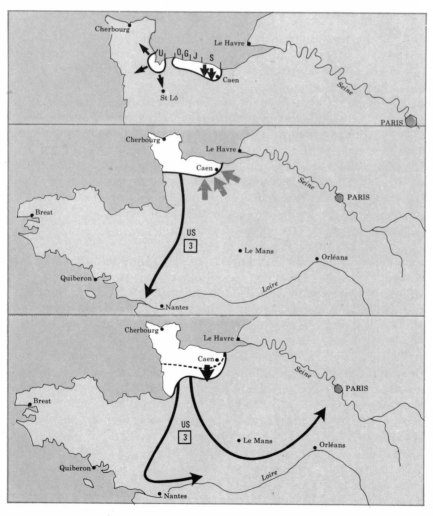

The plan evolves
The sequence of maps, derived from Montgomery's own sketches, shows the development of his strategic concept. The initial bridgehead was to be held, attracting the main German effort to its eastern flank, in order to facilitate a breakout from the west flank and an envelopment of the German army.

Final manoeuvres
Somewhere on the English coast, Tedder, Eisenhower and Montgomery cast a critical eye over one of the final, and critical, beach-assault exercises.

of 5 US Corps (OMAHA) would have to make every effort to join up with 7 US Corps in the south-facing cordon, and maintain the link with the western flank of the British forces. Above all, it would be the responsibility of Second British Army to exert maximum and continuous pressure on the Germans, to endeavour to attract their reserves as they arrived at the front, and thus diminish the strength of enemy counter-attacks on the western flank of the bridgehead. While First US Army was battling in two directions, and until Cherbourg had fallen and the peninsula was clared, Second British Army *had* to attract, and hold, the greater part of the German offensive divisions.

Up to this point, there could be no source of contention between the senior commanders of the higher command. Next came Montgomery's master plan for the further development of the campaign, and I will later recount the explanation as he made it to me in outline in London (at his flat by the HQ offices in St. Paul's School) and again

A major problem *(left and facing page). Well before the invasion was launched, continuous Allied bombing of German production, storage and transportation facilities had created serious fuel shortages, and in an effort to conserve its meagre resources for the mobile armoured divisions, the German army found itself forced to utilize horses, bicycles, handcarts and any other means of transport available.*

when we were compiling his detailed account together in Germany after the war. He had no doubts about the outcome in Normandy, and he confirmed that the planners should adopt as a yardstick the assumption that the Allies would reach the line of the River Seine by D+90 days provided that the post-assault phase was skilfully handled.

The German defences of the 'Western Wall' had little depth, and the violence of our assault he thought would break through them. On the Channel coast and in Brittany, the infantry divisions that were fully equipped first-line formations totalled twelve, of which only two were on the intended invasion frontage. The other divisions were on lower establishments, in a relatively static defence role. They would fight vigorously in their own local areas, but had very restricted power of mobility for manoeuvre. Even first-line infantry were slow movers because the majority of their artillery and transport was horse drawn: the German Army, to conserve vehicle fuel, relied on rail transport for strategic moves of infantry formations, and it was planned that the Allied air interdiction programme would deny them railway transit. There were four first-line divisions in Brittany: if they were moved to Normandy, *en route* they would have to run the gauntlet of our air attacks.

First-line infantry divisions of Fifteenth Army, if sent to Normandy, would have to move by long circuitous routes, because by D-Day all bridges over the Seine west of Paris would be destroyed, and road movement would be attacked from the air and hampered by French Resistance acts of sabotage on road bridges and bottlenecks.

The main threat to our assault would be the three Panzer Divisions (12SS, 21 and Lehr), all of which were south of the Seine. But since

we knew from ULTRA that Hitler was averse to moving 12SS and Lehr nearer to the coast, only 21 was likely to come into action on D-Day unless some last-minute changes were made by the Führer.

With this background, Montgomery argued that once the bridgehead was firmly established, the next priority was to seal off the Brittany Peninsula as a prelude to securing its ports, which meant that the Allies required to make territorial gains on the west flank with all speed. This would involve an offensive from the west flank by First US Army and by Third US Army, which would follow it into Normandy. On the eastern (British) flank, the capture of terrain was not so pressing from the point of view of the army and administrative requirements, but it *was* rated as essential by the air forces because, as already mentioned, the close *bocage* terrain of Normandy was generally unsuitable for rapid airstrip construction, whereas the area south of Caen on the general line Falaise–Argentan, and to the east of it, was flat and open.

From consideration of the immense strategic importance of Caen, Montgomery anticipated that the Germans would react violently, at the expense of the rest of the bridgehead, to any major offensive by the Allies in the area of the town. It was the centre at which the main road and rail communications from the east and southeast converged, and thence led to the Cherbourg Peninsula and to Brittany. Moreover, reserves sent south from Fifteenth German Army, by whatever route they followed (assuming that there would be no bridges usable over the Seine west of Paris), would reach the combat zone through Caen, and the same applied to reinforcements brought up from farther afield, for the rail and road bridges over the Loire were also to be destroyed.

Some time late in March or early in April 1944 I made a sketch, which I retained in my records, of Montgomery's thinking at that time. The main points are that at this stage he was concerned with:

(a) The rapid capture of Cherbourg.

(b) The need to draw the main German defensive efforts to the Caen area, in order to help Bradley in his threefold role in the Cherbourg Peninsula.

(c) The need to cut off Brittany quickly, in order to secure its ports.

(d) The possibility that by making the breakout on the American front to the Biscay coast, a departure point would be provided for an eastern drive along the Loire. If his assumption about the strategic importance of Caen were to prove correct, it seemed logical to attempt a rapid encirclement of German Seventh Army up to the Seine.

Montgomery's original master plan drawn up April 1944

▪▪▪▪ Establishment of bridgehead and capture of Cherbourg

▪■▪■ Breakout by First US Army while Commonwealth troops attract main German defensive effort to Caen

■ ■ Main German effort

▪▪■▪ Envelopment of German Seventh Army by Third US Army

➤ Commonwealth forces eastward drive to line up on Seine

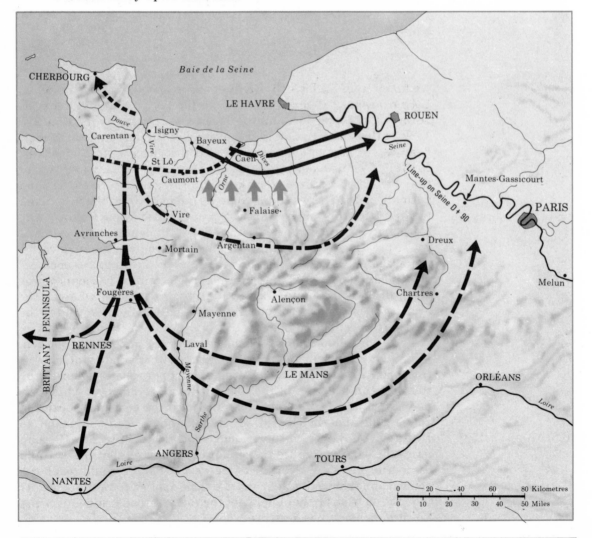

Having reached this stage in his thinking, Montgomery found himself on the horns of a dilemma. On the one hand, the first elements of an attractive plan pointed to an overall operation in the Normandy Lodgment Area, which would pivot on Caen; on the other hand, there remained the problem of the air forces' requirements in the region of Falaise–Argentan, south and southeast of Caen.

There were three Panzer Divisions in Normandy plus one astride the Seine, and if the Germans were to react as Montgomery envisaged, the question was whether the build-up of Allied forces in the British sector would be fast enough to concentrate for a thrust of some thirty-seven miles to Argentan – or even to Falaise, lying about twenty miles inland. The problem then would be that if such an Allied offensive were found to be possible, a long salient would be created – vulnerable on both flanks unless First US Army were to conform on the west flank (thus compromising the rapid seizure of

Montgomery's master plan as presented on 7 May 1944

▪▪▪▪ Establishment of bridgehead and capture of Cherbourg

▪▪▪ Breakout by First US Army while Commonwealth troops attract main German defensive effort to Caen

━━ Main German effort

▬ ▬ ▬ Envelopment of German Seventh Army by Third US Army

➜ Commonwealth forces eastward drive to line up on Seine

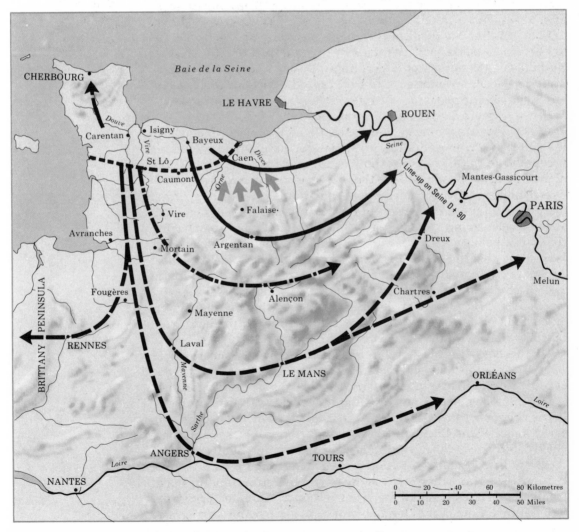

Brittany), while on the east flank considerable forces would be required, but could only be found by weakening the strength of the main drive southwards.

Certain it was that *two* viable offensives, one by First US Army to cut off Brittany, and the other by Second British Army to capture the area Falaise–Argentan, could not be made concurrently in the early stages of the invasion. The Allies would not have the strength nor the required logistical back-up to support both.

The more Montgomery pondered over this problem, the more convinced he became that in the longer term the Allies would above all need port facilities and sheltered waters for unloading ships. He took into account that the need of 'airfield country' was desirable, but could hardly be called, in comparative terms, vital, since the Allied air forces already enjoyed such a degree of mastery of the air.

The problem became that of gaining acceptance of his plan by the air forces. Montgomery hoped to capture Caen on D-Day or very soon afterwards, but saw little hope of getting much farther. If he announced that the pivot of the operation would be Caen, the air forces commanders, and particularly Air Chief Marshal Tedder, Eisenhower's deputy, would certainly refuse to accept it and his draft master plan would have to be scrapped – without there being any apparent alternative which offered the same prospect of success.

When we were discussing this problem of the air forces together, after the war, Montgomery told me that he felt obliged to make to his colleagues a presentation of his master plan which would be acceptable to the air forces without sacrificing his basic conception of the strategy to be adopted. He therefore had a second map prepared which indicated that Second British Army would pivot on Argentan, and advance thence to the west of Paris with the US armies making a much wider swing up to the east side of the city. I must emphasize that when he discussed this version of the master plan, he made it very clear that he could not forecast how quickly the Falaise–Argentan area could be cleared, since it would depend on the strength and speed of the German reaction to the assault and subsequent manoeuvres. He also reminded his colleagues that he had never failed in the past to endeavour to meet the air force requirements and that he would continue to do so.

On this basis, the master plan was approved by all concerned.

My impression was, and remains, that though Montgomery was entirely sincere in his statements, he thought that short of a miracle – such as a complete German collapse – there was little hope of British Second Army reaching Argentan, or even Falaise, in the early stages of the Battle of Normandy. But it will be seen that he made determined efforts very soon after D-Day, and again later. In the event the German opposition proved too strong for us.

In retrospect, I believe that many of the misunderstandings and troubles which, as we shall see, occurred later, were due primarily to a failure on the part of a number of senior commanders to grasp

Sir Arthur Tedder
The Air Chief Marshal's known opposition to any strategy which did not incorporate very early seizure of terrain suitable for the rapid construction of airfield facilities was to prove a major problem for Montgomery in obtaining full approval for his plan for the campaign.

the fundamental concept of Montgomery's strategy. In Montgomery's entourage we were trained to regard his master plan as a framework *within which* both he and his senior subordinates would conduct their detailed operations. Montgomery was always thinking two jumps ahead of current operations: his philosophy was to establish a forward plan which he was confident he could follow whatever the reaction of the enemy might be, and which could not be upset by any tactical measures which might be adopted during the course of the battle.

Before a battle it was his custom to ensure that all officers and men concerned in it knew exactly what was required of them. In his thinking, if once his troops were required to alter their objectives there would arise confusion and misunderstandings, with the danger of a muddle. No commander can afford to risk uncertainties and in Montgomery's view a good plan was one which could not be upset by enemy counter-measures.

His plan provided for a bridgehead in Normandy and the isolation of Cherbourg, followed by a major offensive against Caen designed to commit the major part of the German defensive effort in the British sector and so pave the way for an *American* breakout in the western sector and a subsequent encirclement of the German Seventh Army. His only specifically dated objective was that the Allies would be lined up along the Seine by D+90.

The 'Phase-line' Controversy

During the planning period in London, five American staff officers were working with us – the most senior of which was the US deputy to myself. There came the day when he told me that American staff procedure for the presentation of a major pre-planned offensive required a phase-line map. This meant preparing a map of Normandy and Brittany and marking on it the anticipated progress, from D-Day to our arrival at the River Seine, at intervals of, say, 15, 20, 25, 35 and 60 days. I explained that Montgomery had told us to assume that the Allies would reach the line of the River Seine on D+90, and that an invasion exercise of the magnitude and complexity of OVERLORD was subject to so many imponderables that to guess its progress on a day-to-day basis was neither practical nor helpful.

Next day my deputy came back to say that HQ First US Army *had* to have a phase-line map, but that it would be regarded purely as an indication of the likely development of operations. He showed me a provisional marked map, and asked whether it would suffice. The map showed that by D+20 the Allied front line would form an arc from the River Orne to Avranches on the Atlantic coast of the Cherbourg Peninsula; for D+35 the line was drawn from the River Dives, east of Caen, through Argentan and Le Mans to Nantes on the estuary of the Loire, and so on.

I remember saying that the map could prove misleading, but I undertook to show it to Montgomery which would at least enable my deputy to inform General Bradley that the matter had been referred to the Commander-in-Chief. He was clearly relieved.

The next day was a Sunday, and Montgomery asked me to join him that afternoon at his flat by St. Paul's. It was a favourite time for him to have a quiet chat with one or other of his entourage about the progress we were making and the problems that were concerning us. On this occasion I showed him the map and asked him what to do about it. I had no idea who had drawn it and shared Montgomery's view that such maps were too speculative to be of any practical value, but did not want it to become the subject of a *malentendu* between us and our US colleagues. Montgomery gave me back the map and said, in effect, that I should make it quite clear that he did not wish to be associated with such guesswork.

I put this across as tactfully as possible to my American colleague, and asked him particularly to explain to his General that Montgomery preferred not to put his name to the map. He said that it was only a staff formality anyway. But, alas, the map was recorded in the presentation to the American War Department in Washington and, more importantly, General Eisenhower and Air Chief Marshal Tedder had copies. Only many years later did it become clear that it was not General Bradley who had demanded a phase-line forecast, but the air force planners who were working with the First US Army staff. Bradley, like Montgomery, had no time for speculative forecasts, particularly in an operation as complex as the invasion of Normandy, and consequently Montgomery's retention of the forecast maps – borne out of his overriding concern that the air force planners should not block acceptance of the invasion plan – led almost inevitably to a serious misunderstanding between Bradley and Montgomery.

There came the time, in July 1944, when Tedder – backed by Morgan – began to criticize Montgomery's conduct of operations in Normandy, and even suggested to Eisenhower that he should approach Prime Minister Churchill about replacing Montgomery since the Normandy bridgehead was in danger of reaching a deadlock. The failure to achieve the rate of progress indicated on the phase-line map was quoted as evidence in support of their misgivings. Perhaps the greatest irony was that this rumpus occurred in the period 20–25 July, just as the master plan was about to pay off.

Because this troublesome 'forecast' map subsequently appeared in Montgomery's book *Normandy to the Baltic* – complete with the phase-lines which, through an oversight, were not removed prior to publication as had been the intention – it has unfortunately misled many conscientious students of the Normandy campaign.

The record can now be set straight: phase-lines never at any time had any place in Montgomery's plan. His one and only specifically dated objective was that the Allied armies should be formed up in

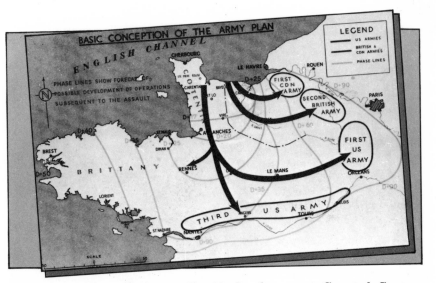

Controversial map
Lt.-Gen. Omar Bradley (left), Senior Commander, U.S. Ground Forces, was destined to become deeply involved in a serious and long-lasting misunderstanding with Montgomery over the phase-line map (right) which showed the possible development of operations after the opening assault on the Normandy coastline.

line at the River Seine on D + 90. In the event General George Patton, commanding Third US Army, arrived at the Seine well ahead of schedule – on D + 75.

One further point which must be emphasized is that the version of the battle which Montgomery had in his mind all along was that outlined in his original presentation of April 1944 and not that presented in London on 7 May, 1944. He knew full well that the German Seventh Army would at all costs deny the Caen area to the invaders and that, if this supposition were to be borne out by events, the enemy would be unable to redeploy quickly enough to hold back the American forces breaking out from the western flank.

But in our informal discussions during late March 1944 Montgomery did raise the possibility of the Germans deciding to withdraw before our onslaught – abandoning Brittany in order to cordon off the Allied invasion in northwestern France along the Loire and Seine. Were the Germans to react in this way, the encirclement plan could partially fail, because the enemy could use ferries by night in order to evacuate Normandy. This possibility obviously worried Montgomery: he wanted to encircle the German Seventh Army. Finally, he told me on 1 April, 1944, a date which I preserved in my *aide-mémoire*, that his sole object was to win an overwhelming victory in Normandy, which he truly believed could be achieved, although not, perhaps, if the master plan were altered to suit the air forces. He added that it was already apparent that the Anglo-American air forces had established such a degree of mastery in the air that they could continue for a while to maintain this status, even if it was necessary for several types of aircraft to return to UK bases for refuelling during the early phases of the invasion.

His argument was proven justified in the event. Despite the lack of airfields in northwestern France, never has any army received such magnificent air cover, air support and air battle co-operation, as was the case in Normandy.

OPERATION BODYGUARD: THE DECEPTION PLAN

In order to clarify the important question of the master plan it has been necessary to depart from the chronological sequence of the story, which is now resumed at 1 February, when the initial assault plan and date were agreed by the Combined Chiefs of Staff.

The preparatory operations for OVERLORD were a vital part of the overall plan, and the utmost care and vigilance were needed to keep them a secret from the enemy. The Deception Plan was designed to mislead the Germans about the place and date of the proposed invasion of Western Europe, since it was impossible to hide from them that preparations were being made for such an operation.

The first part of the plan was intended to indicate that the Allied campaign would begin with an attack on Norway. Camps were set up near several Scottish ports and in Northern Ireland, in which skeleton detachments maintained signs of activity for the benefit of any German air photographic sorties in those areas. A fictitious 'Fourth Army HQ' was simulated in Scotland by considerable wireless traffic, and training exercises were also indicated by wireless messages that included carefully prepared indiscretions pointing to preparations for operations in Norway. This activity continued until July, in the hope of discouraging any German withdrawals from Scandinavia.

We learned later that Hitler had at one stage considered Norway and even Denmark as possible targets for diversionary operations. The main effort, however, was put into convincing German intelligence that the principal Allied thrust would be made in the Pas de Calais, sometime in the second half of July – about 45 days later than the real D-Day. To add credence to information passed through double agents and other underground channels, the troops actually located in eastern and southeastern England were made to appear vastly more numerous by erecting dummy camps, and by maintaining

The deceivers
At close quarters their slightly sagging forms, supporting rods, and lack of fine detail, reveal these dummy tanks, ships and lorries for what they are, but on aerial photographs these elements in the complex deception plan appear totally convincing and lent credibility to the Allied planners' efforts to persuade German intelligence that an entire American army was being assembled in Kent.

a high intensity of wireless traffic to and from nonexistent formations. The development of camps, roads, tracks, craft launching ramps and airfields was carried out openly. Dummy landing craft were assembled in the Cinque Ports and Thames Estuary, and dummy gliders were made conspicuous on various airfields, particularly in Kent. By planned wireless deceptions, the Germans were given to understand that an American Army Group HQ, comprising two assault armies, under General George Patton, was located in Kent; and the General himself was persuaded to be seen in the area, with his conspicuous white dog!

The overall contribution of the Deception Plan cannot be precisely quantified, but there is no doubt at all that it achieved a remarkable degree of success. As far as I am aware, Hitler and his immediate entourage never seriously wavered in their belief that the main Allied assault would be made in the Pas de Calais until late in the month of July. To maintain this conviction the plan continued in operation until well into July, and the best measure of its influence was perhaps the fact that Hitler continued to regard the Normandy landings as a diversionary operation until it was too late to send effective reinforcements from Fifteenth Army to save Seventh Army from its fate.

Considered in conjunction with other Allied measures taken on on D−1 and D-Day, the Deception Plan certainly added to the confusion which resulted in the German High Command's slow reaction to the first news it received about the landings in Normandy. To this may be added that the Allied mastery in the air over the Channel was of capital importance in the last days before the assault; the Luftwaffe made but few hasty reconnaissance sorties over the English harbours and, as late as 4 June, just two days before the invasion, Admiral Krancke (naval commander of the Channel ports area) reported that it appeared doubtful whether the Allies had as yet assembled their full invasion fleet.

Tactical strike
R.A.F. bombers of Second Tactical Air Force head for home after making a daylight raid on the big steelworks at Caen.

THE PREPARATORY OPERATIONS

Apart from the contribution made by the strategic bomber raids on German oil installations and industrial centres, the air forces' preparatory operations may be divided into three prolonged air campaigns directly related to paving the way for OVERLORD.

The first aim was to create and sustain complete mastery in the air over northwestern Europe. Secondly, there was the 'interdiction' programme, the term given to the disruption of the railway system in Belgium and in northern and western France, together with the destruction of rail and road bridges over the Seine and the Loire, in order to disrupt the movement of troops and stores. The third aim was to weaken the enemy's coastal defences in the Normandy assault areas.

The result of the Allied Combined Bomber Offensive on the enemy's aircraft production had not put an end to output from the very dispersed factories, many of which were underground, but they were prevented from achieving anything approaching their full potential. At the same time the diversion of manpower and equipment for the home air defence system in Germany was of importance. The greatest havoc was achieved as a result of attacks on enemy airfields, ground installations and radar, together with the destruction of enemy aircraft on the ground and in the air. Admiral Krancke deplored that by the end of May 1944 the enemy 'had almost complete mastery of the air'.

A measure of the complexity of OVERLORD was that the interdiction programme had to be planned in a manner which would not compromise the Deception Plan. Fortunately it was possible to bring the railway system in Belgium and northern, western and much of central France to a virtual standstill, without having to make numerous raids in the Normandy area as compared with the vast number of strikes north of the Seine, and around (but not in) Paris, and also as far east as the main routes which followed the general

Night sortie
This unusual photograph, taken during the night of 4/5 May during an attack on the Mailly tank depot, shows an R.A.F. Lancaster silhouetted against the glare of fires as it flies low across the towering columns of smoke.

line of the Rhine. One German report recovered, dated 3 June, stated that the Reichsbahn (National Railway) Authorities were seriously considering whether it was even worth trying to attempt further repair work. On road defiles, all but three bridges over the Seine west of Paris had been destroyed before D-Day, and the remaining three did not survive much longer; the bridges over the Loire from its estuary to a point some miles southeast of Orleans were also wrecked. The air action of the interdiction programme was supplemented by courageous acts of sabotage by the Resistance Groups in France and Belgium, and it is a tribute to their discipline, and the maintenance of communications with London, that they did not operate in the area of Normandy or Brittany because of our Deception Plan, even though they did not, of course, know when or where the Allied landings would take place.

The plan to weaken the enemy's coastal defences had also to be dovetailed into the Deception Plan. This was facilitated by our knowledge that all air strikes were reported to a collation centre in Berlin. Each report gave an estimate of the number of Allied aircraft involved and the tonnage of bombs dropped. When the Army planners requested an attack on gun emplacements, rearward artillery positions, military installations and other targets in the Normandy area, they had also to select with the air force planners *two* military

The hidden enemy
The twisted wreckage of a locomotive stands as a silent tribute to the courage of the men and women of the Resistance Movement. In addition to sabotaging rolling stock, the underground fighters made a significant contribution to the inter- diction programme (see map) by blowing up key bridges and other targets in northern France.

Hit – but deadly

Despite the smoke and flame pouring from his wing, the pilot of this B-17 Flying Fortress has held station long enough for his bombardier to release his load of high explosives on Berlin.

* Sabotage
* Allied Bombing

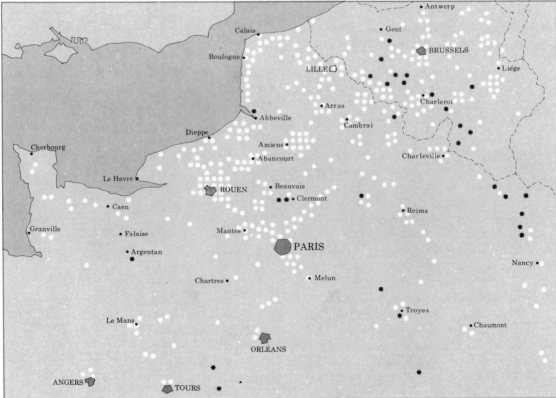

targets in the Pas de Calais zone. The air force planners then arranged with their Operations colleagues for two raids to be made in the north, to compensate for one on Normandy, and for the tonnage of bombs dropped also to be in the same two-to-one ratio.

An idea of the tremendous effort exerted by the combined Allied air forces from mid-March up to the immediate pre-D-Day programme may be judged from the fact that over 200,000 sorties were flown during the period, and nearly as many tons of bombs were released on enemy targets.

The cost was high. Some 2,000 aircraft were lost, along with most of their crews, but the determination of the Allied air forces never wavered and the combined air offensive proved to be a remarkable example of co-ordinated planning.

Preparations for Operation NEPTUNE

Throughout the preparatory operations phase, the Royal Navy worked in close partnership with Coastal Command of the Royal Air Force, the aim being to prevent German submarines and surface craft from penetrating the waters where Allied shipping movements were taking place, and particularly to frustrate any attempt to enter the English Channel. Air reconnaissance and offensive sorties by our naval craft covered the seas around the British Isles and areas as far north as the transit area between Norway and the Atlantic to intercept and prevent the passage of submarines to the key German base at Brest or to the eastern and western entrances to the English Channel. Coastal Command flew some five thousand sorties in the ten weeks prior to D-Day, while an intensive mine-laying programme was carried out by the Royal Navy and RAF Bomber Command with the main concentrations being laid off the Dutch coast, Calais, Boulogne, Le Havre, Cherbourg and Brest.

Admiral Ramsay's greatest problem, however, lay in the pressing need to gather together and train, in the space of only a few months, the thousands of additional officers and crewmen who would be needed on D-Day to man the armada of assault craft and take charge of the various specialist beach parties.

On 26 May, those troops taking part in the assault on the first three tides were moved to special camps near their ports of embarkation, where they were fenced in together with canteen and other administrative workers – completely isolated from the outside world. Briefing was carried out so that every individual knew precisely what his task would be. Models and maps were provided (with fictitious names but otherwise correct in detail); but no-one was told whereabouts in France they would be landed. Only after the invasion fleet had put to sea were the genuine beach assault maps issued.

Considerable drama preceded the final decision about the date of D-Day. Suffice it to say that having originally been fixed for 5 June,

Operation OVERLORD

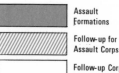

	Assault Formations
	Follow-up for Assault Corps
	Follow-up Corps

Just before D-Day, the entire invasion force transferred from holding camps around the country to the carefully planned assembly areas. It was a huge logistical operation and one requiring complete security if the vital element of surprise was not to be lost.

ALLIED EXPEDIETIONARY AIR FORCE
Air Chief Marshal Sir T Leigh-Mallory RAF
Major-General Hoyt Vaudenberg USAAF

Second Tactical Air
Force
Air Marshal Sir A
Coningham RAF

US Ninth Air Force
Lieut-General Lewis
Brereton (later Major-
General Hoyte
Vandenberg)
Allied Strategic Air
Force
Air Chief Marshal Sir
A Hams RAF
Lieut-General
J Doolittle USAF
Bomber Command RAF
RAF Coastal Command
Air Chief Marshal Sir
W Sholto Douglas

RAF 2, 83, 84, 85, 38,
and 46 Groups
Including French, Polish,
Dutch, Australian,
New Zealand, Canadian,
Norwegian, Czech, Belgian
and Newfoundland
squadrons.

US 9 and 19 Tactical
Air Command. US 9 Bomber
Command. US 9 Troop
Carrier Command.

US 8 Air Force
US 8 Fighter Command
Including Australian,
French, Polish and
Rhodesian squadrons.

15, 16, 18, 19 Groups
Four Squadrons US Navy
Including Australian,
New Zealand, Norwegian,
Czech and Polish squadrons.

ALLIED NAVAL COMMAND EXPEDITIONARY FORCE
Admiral Sir B Ramday

WESTERN NAVAL TASK FORCE
Rear-Adm. A Koch USN

EASTERN NAVAL TASK FORCE
Rear-Adm. Sir P Vian RN

Bombarding Forces

Directing Battleships
HMS Nelson USS Augusta
HMS Bellona
Force A (UTAH)
USS Nevada
HMS Erebus
Five cruisers
Dutch gunboat
Eight US destroyers
Force C (OMAHA)
USS Texas
USS Arkansas
Three US cruisers
Eight US destroyers
Three British destroyers

Directing Battleships
HMS Rodney and Two
Cruisers
Force K (GOLD)
Four British cruisers
Dutch gunboat
Twelve destroyers
Polish destroyer
Force E (JUNO)
Nine British destroyers
Norwegian destroyer
French destroyer
Force D (SWORD)
HMS Warspite
HMS Ramillies
HMS Roberts
Four British cruisers
One Polish cruiser
Ten British destroyers
One Polish destroyer
Two Norwegian destroyers

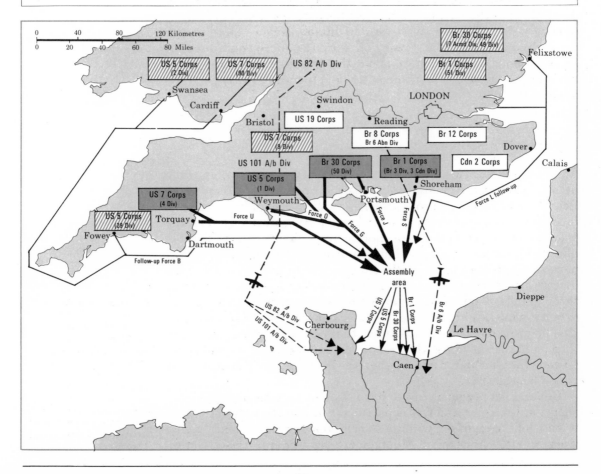

it was postponed 24 hours owing to the highly adverse weather conditions. At 0430 hours on 5 June, the final order was issued: D-Day would be Tuesday, 6 June. By this time some ships and craft, coming from the more remote ports in Scotland and northern England, were already at sea. They had to slow down, or in some cases return to port, to 'mark time' for the extra day. But it was too late to stop the departure of two midget submarines. They had already sailed from Portsmouth to their positions off the French coast where they would act as markers. Each was manned by four officers and an engine room artificer. When they surfaced on the night of D−2 they received news by wireless of the postponement, and submerged at once with the prospect of passing another uncomfortable day on the sea bottom in eleven fathoms.

One final example of the mass of meticulous detail involved in the pre-D-Day planning was the air photographic programme designed to assist accurate navigation to the beaches and to enable troops, once ashore, to pick up their bearings. The coxswain of each landing craft was provided with a photograph of his allotted beaching point, taken 1,500 yards from the shore by an aircraft virtually skimming the sea, while each infantry platoon commander also had an oblique photograph of the terrain inland from his landing area. This degree of support by air reconnaissance was unique. Never before in war had military commanders landed on a foreign shore equipped with so much detailed information about the defensive units and mine-fields facing them, or about the battlefield terrain lying beyond the landing beaches.

The Human Factor

From the middle of May 1944, Montgomery left the completion of the detailed planning to his staff and embarked on a round of visits to the British and American troops assigned to the Normandy assault.

It was a very sound psychological move. His object was to let the soldiers see him and listen to a short address about the task that lay ahead. He sought to gain their confidence. He shunned formal parades – preferring to gather the troops round him while he delivered his message standing on a jeep engine cover. He inspected as many as three parades a day, each attended by some ten thousand men. In essence, what he put across to the American and British soldiers was that he wanted to get to know them; that he had every confidence in them, and that he hoped they reciprocated, because if all had confidence in the plan and in one another, the bursting into a hostile coast would be a success.

General Montgomery must have spoken to considerably more than a million men and it is of particular interest to note the extent to which he 'caught on' with the Americans. In this context, I quote from a letter written to Montgomery by General Bedell-Smith,

Boosting morale
In the months before D-Day Montgomery visited military installations and factories throughout the country in order to achieve the unified effort he believed was essential for success. Here he inspects one of the U.S. ships designated for service in the Western Task Force.

Eisenhower's Chief of Staff, in June 1944:

'Confidence in the high command among the US troops is absolutely without parallel. Having spent my life with American soldiers, and knowing only too well their innate distrust of everything foreign, I can appreciate far better than you what a triumph of leadership you have accomplished in inspiring such feeling and confidence.'

In addition, Montgomery was invited to visit armament factories where he was able to talk to those working on equipment for the armies. He addressed meetings of railway workers, dockers and workers in other industries directly involved in supplying and transporting the weapons and stores which were a vital back-up to the soldiers in the field. His theme was, in simplest terms, that all had to strive together to achieve success by the armed forces.

It was a massive, and time-consuming, exercise but one which Montgomery firmly believed to be of the utmost importance. Morale and confidence are factors which cannot be quantified, but there can be no doubt that Montgomery's round of personal addresses had an important and lasting effect on the troops about to go into battle.

THE DETAILED PLAN OF ASSAULT

On 7 April, 1944, Montgomery assembled the General Officers of the Allied armies, and explained to them in detail his master plan for the campaign. In his exposé he expressed the hope that the city of Caen would be secured on D-Day, and stated that it was his object to pivot the whole Allied offensive on the Caen area. He added that if conditions permitted, every effort would be made to extend the initial bridgehead southwards from Caen in order to secure favourable airfield country for the air forces, but inferred that this would be done within the framework of the master plan. The breakout would be launched from the western (US) flank.

On 15 May, a final conference was held at St. Paul's school, London, at which H.M. King George VI was present in addition to Mr. Churchill, Field-Marshal Smuts, the British Chiefs of Staff and members of the War Cabinet. General Eisenhower, the Supreme Commander, made a short introduction, after which Montgomery outlined the intended plan for the Allied assault. Ramsay and Leigh-Mallory then described the naval and air operations. The important point is that Montgomery again propounded his 'threat on the east flank, breakout on the west flank' philosophy which both Eisenhower and Tedder, and other senior SHAEF officers present, heard repeated in formal circumstances. This is important, because it will be seen that in the course of time problems arose at the high command level about the delays experienced in launching the breakout.

The presentation at St. Paul's was made with the aid of a large-scale map of the assault area, mounted before the audience at an angle of about thirty degrees to the floor so that I, acting as Montgomery's assistant, could walk on it in skid-proof socks and point out the various locations and assault lines as they were mentioned.

For the assault, the Western Task Force, comprising First US Army (Lieut.-General Omar Bradley) and the Western US Naval Task Force (Rear Admiral A. G. Kirk USN), was organized as follows:

The OVERLORD assault plan

☐	Corps	
○	Division	
⌵	Brigade/Reg Combat Team	
◣	Armoured Brigade	
○⚐	Airborne Division	

	UTAH Beach	OMAHA Beach
Reference Point on the map	St. Martin-de-Varreville	St Laurent-sur-Mer
Assault Corps	7 US (Maj.-Gen. J. Lawton Collins)	5 US (Maj.-Gen. L. Gerow)
Leading Division	4 US & Rangers	1 US
Follow-up Divs	Part 90 US	29 US
Build-up Divs	9, 79 & 90 US	2, 2 Armoured US

The Eastern Task Force, comprising Second British Army (Lieut-General Sir Miles Dempsey) and the Eastern Naval Task Force (Rear Admiral Sir Philip Vian RN), was organized as follows:

	GOLD Beach	JUNO Beach	SWORD Beach
Reference Point on the map	Mont Fleury	Courseulles-sur-Mer	Lion-sur-Mer
Assault Corps	30 (Lieut.-Gen. Bucknall)	1 (Lieut.-Gen. J. Crocker)	1
Leading Div.	50	3 Canadian	3
Follow-up Divs	7 Armoured	4SS Bde	1SS Bde
Build-up Divs	49	Part 51	Part 51

To the assault order of battle must be added the three airborne divisions, which were to land on the flanks of the seaborne troops. The availability of transport aircraft and of glider pilots limited the initial lift to two brigades of a British division, with the third brigade to be flown in later, and the greater part of two American divisions, with the remainder to follow.

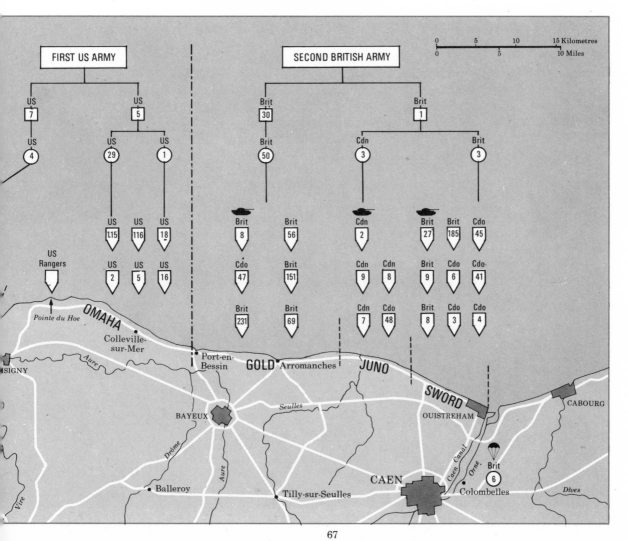

The 6 British Airborne Division was to land in the Caen area during the night of D−1/D and it was decided that 82 US and 101 US should land in the Cherbourg Peninsula: 82 US to the west of UTAH beach in the area of Ste-Mère-Eglise, and 101 US some ten miles west of the town. Montgomery and Bradley were insistent that without the help of airborne divisions the UTAH attack would have to be abandoned, but Air Marshal Leigh-Mallory strongly objected to the operation. He persisted in the opinion that up to 60 per cent casualties, or more, in aircraft and airborne troops might be expected, and emphasized that it was not acceptable to route 915 transport aircraft (96 of them towing gliders) across the Cherbourg Peninsula on a moonlit night. The flight path would pass enemy concentrations which would by that time have been alerted. Leigh-Mallory finally appealed to Eisenhower to intervene on his behalf, but after considering the opinions of Montgomery and Bradley, and consulting Air Chief Marshal Tedder, the Supreme Commander accepted responsibility for the operation: he agreed that without the three airborne divisions the whole operation might be seriously compromised, and overruled his Air Commander-in-Chief.

After the landing of First US and Second British Armies, the second 'wave' would comprise Third US Army under the command of Lieut.-General George Patton, and First Canadian Army under Lieut.-General H. Crerar. 2 French Armoured Division was to land with Third US Army, and 1 Polish Armoured Division with Second British Army, which also included 1 Belgian Infantry Brigade, the

Air commanders (above) *Meeting in Normandy – left to right – Air Vice Marshal Harry Broadhurst; Air Marshal Sir Arthur Conningham, and Air Chief Marshal Sir Trafford Leigh-Mallory.*

Air armada (below) *Row upon row of troop-carrying gliders stand in readiness on an airfield in southern England.*

The last word
Dwight Eisenhower pauses to speak to U.S. paratroops as they prepare to board their aircraft for the night drop on the Cherbourg Peninsula. His orders for the day were, 'Full victory – nothing else.'

Royal Netherlands Brigade and two French battalions.

The names for the American beaches, UTAH and OMAHA, were chosen at General Bradley's HQ and given to me by Colonel Muggeridge. I took the British names, GOLD, JUNO and SWORD, from an Army pamphlet which gave a list of code words that could be understood – without any risk of confusion – by men of different nationalities. In the noise of battle, and against a background of heavy radio interference, accurate information would have to be exchanged between operators with accents ranging from Texas to Glasgow.

The assaulting troops with their weaponry were to be loaded into modified passenger ships, and the required number of small 'landing craft infantry' (L.C.I.) carried on their cleared decks or slung from the davits. Some seven miles offshore (eleven miles in the case of the Americans) the troops would embark, be lowered into the sea, and, together with the craft carrying tanks, artillery pieces, rocket mattresses and other equipment, would run in to the shore. All landing craft had square bows forming a ramp section, which was lowered when the craft was aground on the sand. For the initial waves of troops and equipment 4,126 landing craft of all categories, 736 ancillary craft and 864 merchant ships would be involved, to which must be added the 70 block-ships for the break-waters.

When the time came, and in spite of the unpropitious weather, every main essential of the plan was carried out; a remarkable feat of naval command, organization, skill and discipline.

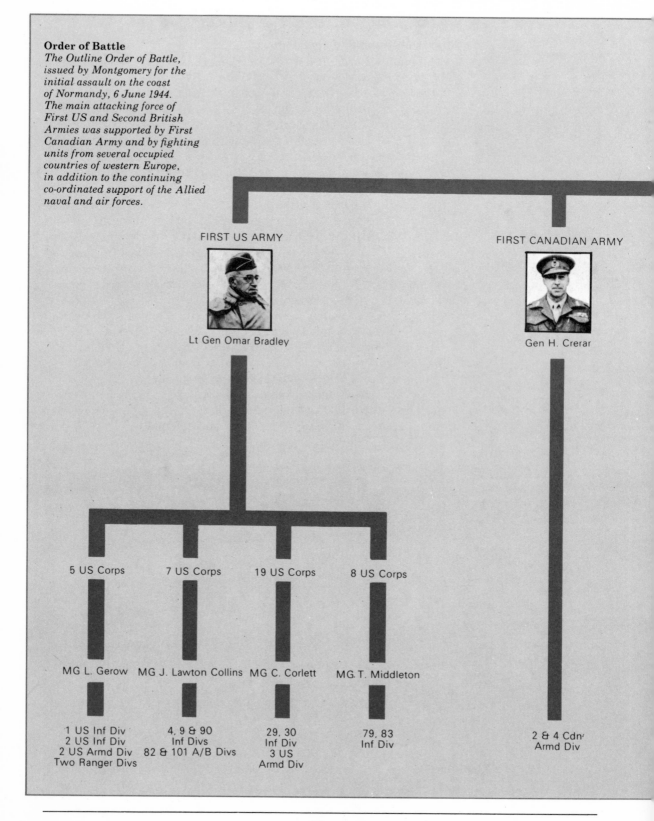

Order of Battle
The Outline Order of Battle,
issued by Montgomery for the
initial assault on the coast
of Normandy, 6 June 1944.
The main attacking force of
First US and Second British
Armies was supported by First
Canadian Army and by fighting
units from several occupied
countries of western Europe,
in addition to the continuing
co-ordinated support of the Allied
naval and air forces.

FIRST US ARMY

Lt Gen Omar Bradley

FIRST CANADIAN ARMY

Gen H. Crerar

5 US Corps

7 US Corps

19 US Corps

8 US Corps

MG L. Gerow

MG J. Lawton Collins

MG C. Corlett

MG. T. Middleton

1 US Inf Div
2 US Inf Div
2 US Armd Div
Two Ranger Divs

4, 9 & 90
Inf Divs
82 & 101 A/B Divs

29, 30
Inf Div
3 US
Armd Div

79, 83
Inf Div

2 & 4 Cdn
Armd Div

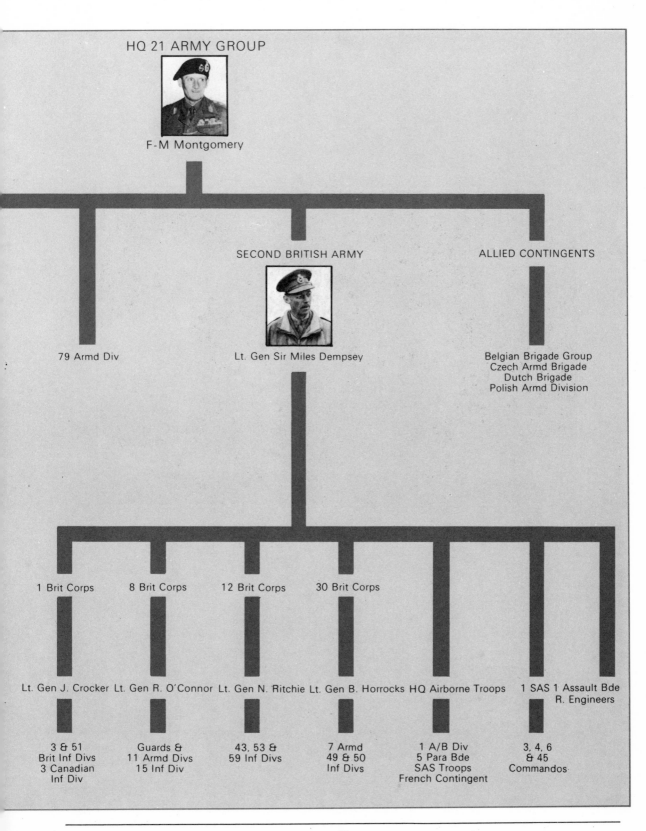

HQ 21 ARMY GROUP

F-M Montgomery

79 Armd Div

SECOND BRITISH ARMY

Lt. Gen Sir Miles Dempsey

ALLIED CONTINGENTS

Belgian Brigade Group
Czech Armd Brigade
Dutch Brigade
Polish Armd Division

1 Brit Corps

8 Brit Corps

12 Brit Corps

30 Brit Corps

Lt. Gen J. Crocker   Lt. Gen R. O'Connor   Lt. Gen N. Ritchie   Lt. Gen B. Horrocks   HQ Airborne Troops   1 SAS 1 Assault Bde
R. Engineers

3 & 51
Brit Inf Divs
3 Canadian
Inf Div

Guards &
11 Armd Divs
15 Inf Div

43, 53 &
59 Inf Divs

7 Armd
49 & 50
Inf Divs

1 A/B Div
5 Para Bde
SAS Troops
French Contingent

3, 4, 6
& 45
Commandos

PART IV

The D-Day Assault

THE AIRBORNE LANDINGS

The invasion commenced when the first groups of vessels, including warships, began the Channel crossing by moving from the forming-up areas, along the mine-swept channels to what was called 'The Spout'. The movement started before darkness fell on D—1 without enemy interference of any sort. We now know that all enemy patrol craft had been ordered to stay in port because of the very bad weather forecast and there was likewise no sign of any Luftwaffe activity. Even so, it is remarkable that the alarm was not raised, as our leading minesweepers could have been observed from the Normandy coast before last light.

While the great armada ploughed its way through heavy seas, battered by strong winds, the Allied measures in preparation for the seaborne assault built up to a climax.

The first air offensive, involving 1,056 aircraft of RAF Bomber Command, was directed against the ten strongest coastal batteries on the invasion frontage. Timing was of the utmost importance. The targets on the extreme flanks, two in the UTAH sector and one to the east of Caen, had to be dealt with no later than 2300 hours on D—1, in order for the bombers to be clear of the areas before the arrival of the first elements of the airborne divisions. 6 British Airborne Division pathfinders – whose task was to mark out the landing areas for the main force – together with a *coup de main* party, were due to land in the Caen area at 0020 hours on D-Day, while 101 and 82 US Airborne Divisions were timed to arrive in the Cherbourg Peninsula at 0130 and 0230 hours respectively. Bomber Command attacked the remaining targets on the invasion frontage between 0315 and 0500, dropping, in all, some 6,000 tons of bombs.

First Foothold in Normandy

The gliders of the *coup de main* party of 6 Airborne Division landed accurately at Bénouville bridge over the Caen canal, rushed the guards and captured the structure intact. Two of the other gliders landed 150 yards from the Ranville bridge over the River Orne and after a short but violent fight this objective was also taken intact.

Maj.-General Gale commanding the 6 Airborne had appreciated that it would be necessary to reinforce the *coup de main* party reasonably quickly, since counter-attacks would surely be made against it if the bridges were captured. The main body of 3 and 5 Brigades was therefore timed to arrive at 0500. Gale's troops had been assigned a fourfold task. First, and most crucial of all, was to take and hold the two key bridges over the Caen canal and the River Orne and so secure the only road north of Caen that ensured a direct line of communication between the seaborne troops due to land on SWORD beach and the airborne troops east of the Orne. Secondly

The pre-emptive strike
This dramatic air photograph, taken on the morning of D-Day, bears witness to the skill of the glider pilots carrying the 'coup de main' party of 6 Airborne Division in their night attack on the bridges over the Caen canal and the River Orne. Sliding to a halt over the soft level ground, the gliders have disembarked their troops almost within firing range of the target.

Sixth Airborne division 5–6 June

 Landing zones

Priority tasks

1 Capture of bridges over Caen canal and River Orne
2 Destruction of Merville battery
3 Destruction of bridges over River Dives

Secondary task

– – – Establish bridgehead for future operations east of Orne

The prime objectives of the bridges over the Caen canal, River Orne, and River Dives, were all captured or blown by the end of D-Day and in the face of fierce opposition the Merville battery (which to Allied surprise had survived heavy bombing on D−1) was also silenced. However, this entire area was bitterly contested until mid-August.

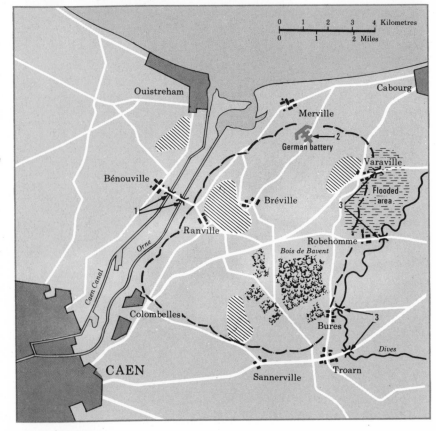

they had to capture and neutralize the powerful battery sited at Merville: even though heavily bombed, the battery was still functioning and was well within range of the landing beach. The third task was to seize and destroy four bridges over the River Dives and its tributaries to prevent enemy reinforcements moving against the eastern flank of the bridgehead; and finally 6 Airborne was to deploy in the Lodgment Area in readiness to develop operations east of the Orne.

By soon after dawn on D-Day, 6 Airborne had accomplished its primary objectives. It was in due course reinforced by seaborne troops, but only after some delay, during which t[...] tinguished itself by repulsing a series of very deter[...] attacks. Thus Montgomery had realized his intentio[...] bridgehead, albeit a narrow one, to the northeast[...] which further operations could be launched when th[...]

The Western Flank

101 US and 82 US Airborne Divisions commenced la[...] and 0230 hours respectively, on the Cherbourg Peninsu[...]

The start of
"The D-Day assault "

[...]e *(left)*
[...]repare
[...]brief
[...]at has
[...]sides.
[...]lace in
[...]
[...]ntan on
14 June.

Return journey *(right)*
Fatigue and relief shows on the faces of these U.S. Army glider pilots as they are transferred by landing craft from the American assault beaches to a larger craft lying offshore. Their initial task completed, they are to return to England to await further orders.

101 was to secure the western end of the narrow causeways running across the belt of flooded ground which ran behind UTAH beach, separated from the shore only by sand dunes. They were then to advance to the River Douve and beyond to capture the town of Carentan, after which a force was to be sent to the east to link up with 5 US Corps fighting their way inland from OMAHA beach. The prime objective of 82 Division, landing farther inland astride the River Merderet, was to seize the town of Ste-Mère-Eglise, and the bridgeheads across the Merderet, in readiness for the thrust which was later to be made by 7 US Corps across the Cherbourg Peninsula to the west coast.

Unfortunately the dropping of the US airborne (parachute) divisions, and the landing of the troop-carrying gliders with them, went badly awry. The approach was made by an indirect route, the flight path running initially southwestwards from the English coast from the area of Portland Bill, and then wheeling eastwards to cross the Cherbourg Peninsula in order to approach the dropping zones from the west. The US troop carriers therefore had a much more difficult navigational task than those of the British RAF aircraft, which flew along a direct path from Littlehampton to the dropping zones northeast of Caen without crossing a wide belt of enemy-held

country. As the American aircraft crossed the west coast of the Cherbourg Peninsula they ran into thick cloud and a barrage of anti-aircraft fire. Maj.-General Maxwell Taylor later reported that the A.A. fire was of 'considerable volume', and that it produced, 'an unfortunate effect upon the pilots who had never seen action before'.

While the cloud did reduce aircraft casualties (only 20 troop-carrying aircraft were lost out of a total of 805 in the operation) it seriously upset navigation, and this factor, combined with the exaggerated evasive action of the pilots, greatly increased the difficulty and hazards of jumping. The troops of 101 Division were scattered over a wide area, and by dawn only 1,100 paratroops had reached their rendezvous points out of a total of 6,600.

82 Division, under the command of Maj.-General Matt Ridgway, had better luck at the outset. The first regiment landed reasonably accurately within three miles of Ste-Mère-Eglise, and the town was captured by 0400 hours. But the remainder of the force was not so fortunate; almost half the 52 gliders carrying guns and signal equipment went astray. As a result, the attempts to seize the bridges of the River Merderet failed, and the division found itself scattered over a wide area of rivers, streams and swamp country garrisoned by the German 91 Division. The American paratroopers, fighting in small groups in this most difficult waterlogged *bocage* country, with very few landmarks and lacking most of their equipment, displayed indomitable courage and initiative. However, the fact that they were scattered over such a wide area had one unforeseen benefit: it confused the German defenders and diverted their attention from the role of counter-attacking the seaborne invaders on UTAH beach.

The 101 Division, as it progressively began to concentrate, found itself in the area between the coast defences and the German 91 Division reserve, where there were few enemy positions. By 0600 hours, though still mustering only one-sixth of its strength, the division was gaining possession of the western exits from the causeways across which the 7 US Corps would advance inland.

The German Seventh Army was remarkably slow in reacting to the situation. The news that paratroops had landed in the Cherbourg Peninsula was received apparently without undue alarm, but as a routine precaution Seventh and Fifteenth Armies were placed on alert. The headquarters of Naval Group West judged that the Allied operations did *not* indicate a major invasion, and decided that patrol craft would not put to sea owing to the unfavourable tide conditions and the prevailing bad weather.

At 0215, Speidel, Rommel's Chief of Staff, was informed by HQ Seventh Army that 'engine noises' could be heard at sea off the coast of the Cherbourg Peninsula, and that ships had been reported by the radar watch at Cherbourg. He relayed this information to Von Rundstedt, but again it was agreed that there was no cause to suspect a major Allied operation.

Reinforcements arrive
This daylight photograph, taken on D-Day, shows support troops pouring into the Cherbourg Peninsula as the massive air operation by U.S. 9th Air Force continues. Tow-planes and gliders circle the landing zone while, at left centre, the first gliders have landed. Wreckage at left and in right foreground highlights the hazards of landing the heavily-laden unpowered gliders.

Coastal radar
The concrete observation tower, surmounted by its radar scanner, was manned by communications specialists and formed part of a continuous line of such stations stretching from Holland to Cherbourg. Of 92 installations, all but 18 had been rendered inoperative by the R.A.F. prior to the invasion.

At 0309 hours, Admiral Krancke, having become more apprehensive, ordered torpedo boat flotillas from Le Havre and Cherbourg to make a sweep into the Baie de la Seine in spite of the weather. The craft from Le Havre did locate some destroyers on the east flank of the Allied invasion fleet, and one British destroyer was damaged in a brief engagement, and yet the Cherbourg sortie returned to port with 'nothing to report'. The Admiral's main concern however was the lack of information from the German radar system, and here events demonstrate the effectiveness of the Allies' efforts to render the chain of radar stations along the Channel coast not only inoperative but also misleading.

The Dummy Invasions

The Germans had confidence that they could not be taken by surprise in the event of an Allied attack from the air or the sea, because the Luftwaffe had established an early warning system based on a line of radar stations roughly ten miles apart from Holland to the Cherbourg Peninsula, backed by a comprehensive inland back-up. Superimposed, there were naval radar stations, which could distinguish ships up to 30 miles from the shore.

But in the period immediately preceding D-Day these stations had been heavily attacked by the RAF with great success. On the night of D—1/D-Day, between Le Havre and Barfleur (a few miles east of Cherbourg), not one single radar installation remained operative; and of the normal ninety-two stations in the coastal chain, only eighteen were serviceable during this vital period. Most of the latter were jammed by specially equipped Allied aircraft and naval craft

Admiral Kranke
The Commander-in-Chief of the coastal defence system, including the few available patrol vessels, photographed on one of his tours of inspection.

circling in the Channel, but a sufficient number located *north* of the River Seine were purposely left unharmed in order that they should pick up and report the decoy 'invasion fleets' code-named GLIMMER and TAXABLE.

As the real invasion fleet ploughed its way across the Channel, the work of the deception planners reached its own climax in a series of decoy operations. To add confusion to the German reading of events, dummy parachute drops were made southwest of Caen; between Dieppe and Le Havre, and in the area west of St-Lô. The dummy paratroopers were each 'armed' with a repeater apparatus which, on landing, gave off the sound of intermittent rifle fire. Simultaneously, clouds of 'window' – fine strips of metal foil – were dropped from aircraft over the Channel to produce, on the few surviving enemy radar receivers, the effect of vast numbers of aircraft heading for the Pas de Calais and the stretch of coast between Le Havre and Dieppe. The deception in this sector was particularly effective and groups of Luftwaffe night fighters spent from 0100 to 0400 hours searching the skies for the phantom invaders.

At sea level, the dummy invasion fleets GLIMMER and TAXABLE were simulated by groups of motor launches in convoy formation, towing balloons carrying radar reflectors and emitting smoke and radar-jamming signals. Lancaster bombers flying overhead in box formation dropped clouds of 'window' to add to the mass of spurious radar readings.

Finally, a number of fast launches carrying highly specialized equipment were dispatched to jam the radar sets installed in the sighting equipment of the guns of the heavy coastal artillery batteries, and to 'feed' distracting readings to the one remaining active radar installation at Cherbourg.

Confusion before the Storm

From around 0300 onwards, further reports began reaching Seventh German Army HQ, and Rommel's Army Group 'B' HQ, of airborne landings in a wide variety of places. Seventh Army reports suggested that the depth of the Allied airborne deployment indicated 'a large-scale enemy assault', and very soon after this the heavy bomber attacks were reported. Shortly after 0600 the start of the Allied naval bombardment at points along the Normandy coast at last convinced the Seventh Army Commander that a major attack was indicated, but in making his report he stated that 'it could be a diversionary attack', and complained that there had been no news from air or sea reconnaissance since daybreak.

The lack of firm decision by the enemy's High Command reflects the leaders' obsession with the idea that the Normandy activity was a diversion to cover a principal assault elsewhere. But the German formations directly facing the Normandy beaches were under no illusions. As early as 0235, Seventh German Army ordered 84 Corps to eradicate the US airborne landings in the Cherbourg Peninsula, employing 91 and 709 Divisions for the purpose, but it was not until 0700 that 21 Panzer Division was released to 84 Corps to assist in dealing with the British airborne troops in the area between the Rivers Orne and Dives. At the time of that order, the first waves of landing craft were already within a few miles of the SWORD landing beach.

Dawn raiders
A group of A-20 'Havoc' light bombers of the U.S. 9th Air Force flies low across the countryside on its way to a target somewhere deep inside France.

The boundary between the German Seventh and Fifteenth Armies ran south from a point on the coast about three and a half miles west of the River Dives, and a small number of British airborne troops were landed by mistake on the Fifteenth Army side of the line. This was reported to Fifteenth Army, and caused some alarm: by 0200 they had asked that 12SS Panzer Division be moved forward from the Lisieux area, but only after a prolonged exchange of messages through normal channels was permission given at 1000 hours by Hitler's HQ (OKW) for the division to advance to a position south of the beach area. At the same time, OKW ordered that the third Panzer division in Normandy – Panzer Lehr – should remain south of Chartres, and that neither 12SS nor Lehr should be committed without direct orders from Hitler.

By 0515 Speidel signalled Von Rundstedt that there were indications of a large-scale Allied operation, but the Field-Marshal was still unconvinced. At 0530, still before daylight, the Eastern (British) Task Force reached its lowering positions, seven miles from the beach, and the heavy naval bombardment opened up. But still it was the airborne attack that occupied the enemy's attention. Two Panzer Grenadier regiments of 21 Panzer Division had joined units of 716 Division in counter-attacks against 6 British Airborne Division and, in the west, 91 and 709 Divisions with a regiment from 915 Division were contesting 82 and 101 US Airborne Divisions, the unintended dispersion of which had greatly magnified the apparent scale of the Allied airborne invasion in the peninsula.

Nautical twilight came at 0550 and soon after, to the noise of the hundreds of fighters providing blanket air cover over the channel and coast areas, and the shattering impact of the naval bombardment, was added the roar of bombers as 8 US Air Force and 9 US Air Force joined the attack. Between 0600 and 0815, 269 medium bombers of 9 US Air Force pounded the German defences on UTAH beach, while some 1,300 Flying Fortresses and Liberators of 8 US Air Force flew in waves of 36 abreast over the other beaches, dropping in all some 3,000 tons of bombs in a sustained attack which was broken off only ten minutes before the first waves of troops hit the beaches.

As the seaborne troops stormed ashore they met fierce opposition; but bitter though the fighting was, it was against a defending army already part broken by the most devastating bombardment ever endured by ground troops. The Atlantic Wall was by no means smashed, but it was weakened and cracked: its communication and supply lines were disrupted, and its defenders were dazed by the ferocity of the opening attack.

THE SEABORNE ASSAULT

Cloud conditions in the early morning of D-Day were not favourable for the US Bomber forces when they swept over the coastal target area, and they were particularly adverse in the OMAHA area. Fearful of releasing bombs on the assault craft approaching the beaches, bomb aimers who could not clearly discern their targets tended to release in the rear of the enemy strong-points. Despite the massive air bombardment by Bomber Command and the US Air Forces, it seemed remarkable that the enemy coast defences had not been more effectively destroyed, and the presence of the Allied warships, with naval observers to control their fire, proved of the utmost importance in the ensuing hours. The bombers had, however, effectively stunned and neutralized the enemy opposition during the crucial period of the assault; they had largely eliminated the rearward fieldworks and many of the minefields and wire entanglements; and had wrecked the defenders' communications network.

Because the actual time of H-hour – when the landing craft were to hit the beaches – was 0630 hours at UTAH and OMAHA, and from 0725 to 0745 on the eastern sector beaches, the timing of the air bombing and naval bombardment operations also varied, which added to the complexity of the planning.

The Western (US) Task Force decided to limit the daylight bombing and shelling of the beach defences to the period from nautical twilight until 40 minutes before H-hour in order to minimize the time during which the defenders would be able to observe the approaching craft and the unloading of troops and vehicles of the first assault wave. The Eastern Task Force on the other hand opted for up to two hours' visual 'softening up' of any German beach defences that had survived previous attacks.

The Assault Technique
The diagram on the facing page shows the essential elements in the assault formation of one brigade group on final approach. The time would be H–30 and the destroyers would have been firing for about ten minutes. Beach defences are now engaged by guns mounted on the flank landing craft.

FLEETS	Destroyer Class
HUNTS	Destroyer Class
L.C.A.	Landing Craft, Assault
M.L.	Motor Launch
L.C.T.	Landing Craft, Tank
L.C.F.	Landing Craft, Flak
A.V.R.E.	Assault Vehicle. Royal Engineers
DD Tank	Duplex Drive Amphibious Tank
L.C.S.	Landing Craft, Support
L.C.G.	Landing Craft, Gun
(A)	Armoured
(R)	Rocket
(HR)	Hedgerow, used to explode mines
(HE)	High explosive
(CB)	Concrete Buster
(M)	Medium
(L)	Large

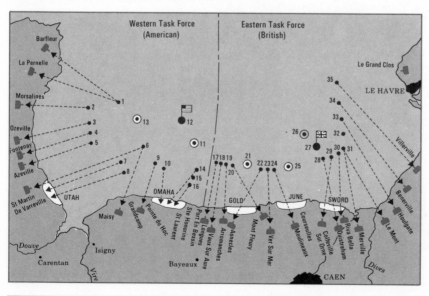

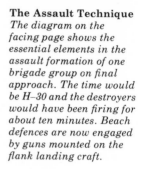

Naval bombardment targets
5.30 a.m. - 8.00 a.m.
on D-day

Batteries
Beaches
Headquarters ships of
Assault Forces
Flagship of
Western Task Force Commander
Flagship of
Eastern Task Force Commander

1	Erebus	19	Emerald
2	Black Prince	20	Orion
3	Tuscaloosa	21	Bulolo
4	Quincy	22	Flores
5	Nevada	23	Belfast
6	Hawkins	24	Diadem
7	Enterprise	25	Hilary
8	Soemba	26	Larges
9	Texas	27	Scylla
10	Glasgow	28	Danae
11	Ancon	29	Dragon
12	Augusta	30	Frobisher
13	Bayfied	31	Arethusa
14	Geo. Leygues	32	Mauritius
15	Montcalm	33	Roberts
16	Arkansas	34	Ramillies
17	Ajax	35	Warspite
18	Argonaut		

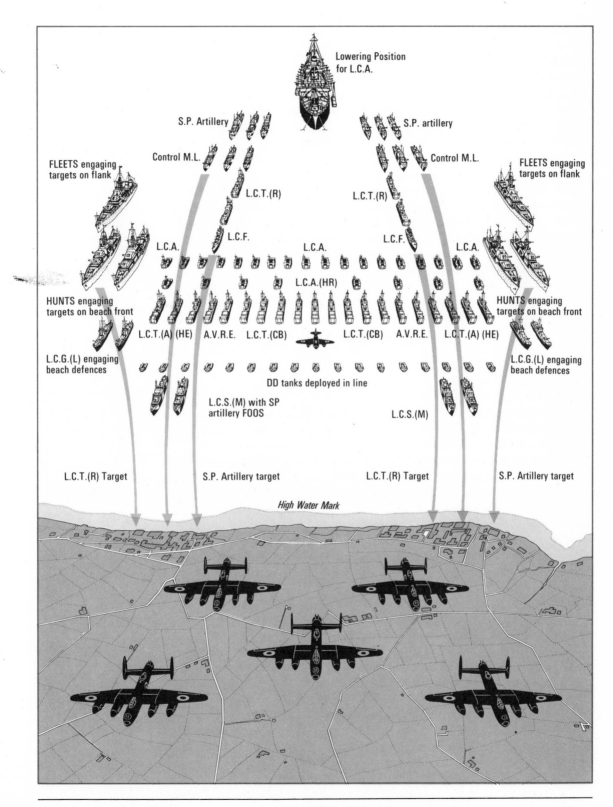

Lowering Position for L.C.A.

S.P. Artillery

S.P. artillery

Control M.L.

Control M.L.

FLEETS engaging targets on flank

FLEETS engaging targets on flank

L.C.T.(R)

L.C.T.(R)

L.C.A.

L.C.F.

L.C.A.

L.C.F.

L.C.A.

L.C.A.(HR)

HUNTS engaging targets on beach front

HUNTS engaging targets on beach front

L.C.T.(A) (HE)   A.V.R.E.   L.C.T.(CB)   L.C.T.(CB)   A.V.R.E.   L.C.T.(A) (HE)

L.C.G.(L) engaging beach defences

L.C.G.(L) engaging beach defences

DD tanks deployed in line

L.C.S.(M) with SP artillery FOOS

L.C.S.(M)

L.C.T.(R) Target

S.P. Artillery target

L.C.T.(R) Target

S.P. Artillery target

High Water Mark

Finally a decision had to be made about the optimum position of the incoming tide, in relation to the time of high tide, for the landing craft to discharge their loads and be ready to withdraw on the outgoing tide for their return trip to the 'parent' vessel. Calculations revealed that the craft would have to complete their run-in not later than three hours before high tide. Thereafter the movement of the tide accelerated at a rate which would leave insufficient time for a vessel to make a quick get-away before the turn of the tide left it stranded.

To deal with underwater obstacles, ideally touch-down of the craft would have been at low tide, but this would have involved a considerably longer run for the troops from the craft to the shore, under direct observation of the defenders. As an insurance against problems with the outer obstacle lines, naval personnel, including skin-divers, were included in the underwater obstacle clearance teams in the leading assault groups.

H-hour at GOLD and SWORD was to be at 0725 hours; but the landings at JUNO were allowed an extra ten to 20 minutes because there were likely to be navigational problems in crossing over the rocky outcrop offshore before reaching the beach.

The Western Task Force

On UTAH beach, one Regimental Combat Team (RCT) of 4 US Infantry Division (equivalent in the British army to three infantry battalions together with supporting arms) led the assault of General Lawton Collins's 7 US Corps. The landing beach was approximately due east of Audouville-la-Hubert and St-Germain-de-Varreville. The D-Day objective was to link up with 82 and 101 US Airborne Divisions, clear the main road from Carentan to St.-Mère-Eglise, and establish bridgeheads over the River Vire and the canal in preparation for the link-up with 5 US Corps from OMAHA. Offshore, a previously undetected minefield caused some casualties at sea, but in general the landing operation went well. The sea conditions were easier than elsewhere, being in the lee of the peninsula, and the troops landed on time, supported by 29 amphibious tanks which had been launched about 5,000 yards offshore. The beach obstacles were cleared with commendable speed, and the build-up began.

Beyond the narrow belt of shoreline sand dunes, the polder-like meadows – up to 3,500 yards wide – had been inundated by breaching the dykes. In places they could be crossed on foot, but in other parts they were under water by as much as four or five feet. They could be crossed by vehicles only along the narrow causeways, of which there were four opposite the landing area – all covered by enemy positions. But 101 Airborne Division was already attacking the defenders at the western exits when the seaborne landing began.

4 Division made initially for Pouppeville, which was attacked at

Heading for UTAH
Eleven miles from the beach, infantrymen of 7 US Corps' 9 Division clamber into their landing craft for the run in. These men formed the second wave of troops to storm UTAH beach, following close behind their colleagues of 79 Div. In one respect at least they were fortunate: the sea was relatively calm. Only a few miles away, US troops heading for OMAHA were being battered by three to four foot waves.

0800 and cleared of enemy by noon, and for Varreville and Audouville. The delays in deployment were caused more by the causeway bottlenecks than by the enemy. The Germans were confused by the dispersion of the scattered airborne troops, who had formed small groups over a wide area and were stoutly fighting their way towards the concentration areas. By mid-morning, the width of the landing area had been extended to 4,000 yards, and 4 Division had advanced some four miles inland. It was opposed by strong forces of 91 German Infantry Division, but, though making good progress, was unable to join up with 82 Airborne Division holding the village of Ste-Mère-Eglise against a German attack from the north.

To the south, some groups of 101 Airborne were holding a counter-attack by 9 German Parachute Regiment, which had been in the Carentan area, but 4 Division managed to link up with HQ 101 Division near Hiesville. Meanwhile, other airborne groups had established positions on the Carentan canal.

At the end of the day, 7 US Corps had been unable to extend the bridgehead to the west, over the Merderet River; there remained a strong enemy pocket to the east and south of St-Mère-Eglise, and they were still some miles from Carentan. Nevertheless, the Corps had established a firm beach-head with room to manoeuvre and the build-up was proceeding most successfully. By nightfall 23,000 men, 1,700 vehicles and 1,700 tons of stores were already ashore.

The Americans go in
*U.S.S. Augusta stands
out starkly against the
skyline as the heavily
laden assault landing
craft head for the beaches.*

Hitting the beaches
Dramatic official U.S. Army/Navy photographs on these pages show the first waves of American soldiers storming ashore at OMAHA beach on D-Day. Without doubt OMAHA was the most difficult of the invasion beaches and for many hours the position there hung on the brink of disaster. Only dogged determination, helped by timely naval support fire, saved the day.

The Desperate Fight for OMAHA

The one sector of the invasion frontage which gave cause for serious concern on D-Day was OMAHA beach, where, for several hours, the situation appeared to hover on the brink of disaster. A number of factors contributed to this, the first being that through a stroke of ill-fortune, 352 German Division, which had been moved from the St-Lô area, was carrying out a full-scale practice of its defence role in the area, so that 5 US Corps ran straight into a fully deployed first-line formation in addition to the expected units of 716 German Coastal Defence Division. Secondly, the air bombing of the sector had been largely ineffective due to cloud conditions. To this must be added that Rear Admiral Hall USN reported afterwards that the assault planning had been at fault in allowing the warships only 40 minutes for the engagement of beach defences before the landings.

The landing beach was within a four-mile sector of coastline which curved gently inland. But the profile of the terrain which confronted the invading troops was the most forbidding on the entire assault frontage. For much of the mile and a half of the landing area there was a rising shingle beach, behind which lay up to 200 yards of marshland extending to the base of a steep grassy bluff that rose to a height of 100 feet or more. In some places, the bluff reached right down to the shingle and rose as high as 200 feet. The bluff was the seaward side of a plateau that extended inland for several miles, to the valley of the River Aure.

There were three belts of obstacles on the soft sand of the tidal flat; the outer belt was roughly 200 yards from the normal high-tide mark and was fully submerged at about half tide. The area at the base of the bluffs was mined and wired, and there were anti-personnel mines on the slopes to the top, in places where men might attempt to

Wall of defence
Cramped and cold, these young German infantry-men take up their firing positions in the complex of concrete walls flanking one of the big gun emplacements.

scale them. The marshland patches were also heavily mined.

There were, however, five relatively narrow valleys or re-entrants along which tracks led up to the plateau, passable – in width and angle of slope – to vehicles. The tracks were mined and each of them was covered by one or more enemy strong-points, which had a field of fire down to the beach entrant; the whole landing area was under observed fire from enemy positions along the top of the bluffs, where there were also observation posts directing artillery fire from batteries in the rear.

Of the five Allied beaches, OMAHA presented the most difficult problem from a *physical* point of view, owing to a combination of the contour of the terrain and the nature of the offshore rocks.

The attack was led by two regimental combat teams; one from the 29 US Infantry Division on the right flank, and the other from 1 US Infantry Division on the left. The latter was a very experienced formation which had taken part in the invasions of Sicily and southern Italy. Two Ranger battalions (commandos) also took part in the assault and their tasks included the capture of Point du Hoe, a formidable dominating feature some three and a half miles west of the landing beach.

As at UTAH, the lowering position was eleven miles off-shore. With H-hour at 0630, only 40 minutes after nautical twilight, the assault craft set off in the darkness. Unlike UTAH, the OMAHA operation took place in more open seas, with waves up to three or four feet high, a contrary wind and a strong tidal current. In the darkness there was confusion in marshalling the landing craft, and those carrying the artillery, amphibious tanks and also the special beach obstacle clearance parties lost station. Of 32 amphibious tanks only five crossed the beach; of 51 tanks carried in landing craft to the shore, eight were 'brewed up' (hit and set on fire) by enemy

Early casualties
Fortunate survivors from one of the landing craft sunk on the run-in to OMAHA beach on D-Day

fire before they had cleared the surf. A number of the artillery pieces proved too heavy for the amphibious lorries carrying them, and the majority capsized.

As the infantry, woefully short of their supporting tanks and artillery, waded ashore they were subjected to a murderous volume of enemy fire, and their task was made more difficult through faulty navigation of the landing craft, which became scattered and, in some cases, landed men of one unit in the middle of another, causing even more confusion. Admiral Hall USN recorded that the crews of the craft, particularly the controllers, had had insufficient instruction and practical training for a manoeuvre of this difficulty. Half the beach clearance teams were delayed, and the majority were landed in the wrong places; they suffered heavy casualties and due to late arrival had no time to deal with most of the obstacles covered by the rising tide. The American command had decided not to use flail (mine-clearing) tanks or assault engineer tanks, but opted for bulldozers instead for the clearance task. Of the 16 bulldozers accompanying the right section of the assault, only two could be put to work on the beach.

The survivors of the initial assault wave were pinned at the water's edge, desperately seeking cover in the shingle banks or at the foot of the bluff while enemy fire continued to sweep the area as the succeeding waves arrived. Admiral Hall's description was of a 'milling mass' of craft arriving while others attempted to withdraw after unloading.

Western Task Force
The troop carriers and support ships of the Western Task Force steam to their positions off the American sector beaches as the invasion of Normandy begins. Barrage balloons, put up to deter enemy air attacks, were superfluous: hardly an enemy aircraft was seen during the landings.

The OMAHA landing had a most inauspicious start, and it was due only to the immense courage and tenacity of the American troops, and the fine example of their leaders, that the costly struggle to gain a foothold was maintained. In spite of uncleared beaches, mines and barbed wire obstacles, small groups of US soldiers braved the storm of enemy fire and began groping their way up the slopes of the bluff. At about 0730 a positive improvement in the whole situation at last came about. Seeing the plight of the troops pinned down by the hail of fire from the bluffs, eight US and three British destroyers closed to the beach at speed – one of them to within 800

OMAHA beach
*The scene on OMAHA
after the initial assault
was one of chaos. The
debris of landing craft
wrecked by enemy fire or
through being capsized on
the run in, lies piled
among the beach-defence
obstacles. Engineers
inspect the scene planning
clearways through the
wreckage for the follow-up
troops and noting equip-
ment and vehicles for
salvage.*

yards. The warships were able to engage the enemy positions by direct fire, and after the agonizing experience of the first hour, during which they had received no effective fire support, the pressure was eased and the troops were able to show their true mettle. By about 0900 some elements had actually reached the top of the bluff and were attacking and eliminating enemy fire positions, while others were attempting to advance towards the villages of Vierville-sur-Mer and St-Laurent-sur-Mer by turning the flanks of the German reserves posted in them. Finally, at about 0930, due to very accurate fire from a destroyer, which knocked out the strong-point covering the track through the hills to Colleville-sur-Mer, a party of 1 US Division stormed the gap.

By 1600 two further regimental combat teams, under 1 US Division, were ashore. Meanwhile, the naval gunfire proved so effective that the German gunners in several strong-points were forced to sur-render, and three more of the five re-entrant tracks were open to the Americans. Reinforcements made rapidly for the plateau, but troops of 352 German Division were fighting stubbornly to defend the villages. On the right, the US troops broke into Vierville, and on the other flank into le Grand Hameau, but could get no farther until more reinforcements arrived next day. In the centre, the main penetration was made between Colleville and St-Laurent. Towards nightfall the position was that the former was virtually surrounded, but in St-Laurent the street fighting continued.

The air forces had been unable to afford any appreciable support because so many radio sets had been sunk, damaged or lost that bomb-line data, and the positions of forward troops, could not be notified.

The day's fighting at OMAHA had been a remarkable achieve-ment by the US infantry and a great credit to the skilful action of the warships supporting them. On the ground, only a few tanks got forward by the end of the day and the infantry units had little field artillery support. Pockets of enemy still held out on the plateau, and

Moving off
An American foot patrol moves off along the beach to reconnoitre the route towards the strongly-held enemy position at Point-du-Hoe, west of OMAHA.

for most of the day had been directing gunfire on to the littered beaches. At the cost of over 3,000 casualties a foothold had been gained, but it was less than two miles in depth at its most forward point. The Rangers had, however, managed to capture Point du Hoe.

By midnight, it was calculated that including beach clearance and other ancillaries, some 33,000 men had been put ashore, but there were heavy losses of landing craft in the process, and the beach obstacles remained only partially cleared until later on D+1.

The situation at OMAHA continued to cause grave anxiety to Bradley throughout the night because had the Germans concentrated a counter-attack force of the calibre of 352 Division, which had proved a stout fighting formation, the Americans would have found it difficult indeed to resist a determined thrust by the enemy. But we were later to learn from intercepted radio reports that HQ Seventh German Army, and Rommel's Army Group HQ, had been informed by the German commander of the defences in the OMAHA area that the Allied landing was under control. Indeed it was not until 1800 hours on D-Day that Rommel learnt of the American progress on the plateau. By this time the only available German reserves in the St-Lô area (a brigade of 716 Division) had been sent on bicycles – there being no other 'transport' available – to the Bayeux sector, where 50 British Division from GOLD beach was threatening the town. Subsequently, two reserve battalions of 352 Division were also ordered to Bayeux, leaving the German 84 Corps with no means of attempting to reverse the position in the OMAHA area.

It is no reflection on 29 US Infantry Division to observe that the previous experience of 1 US Infantry Division in the invasions of Sicily and southern Italy proved invaluable in this, the most critical of the D-Day situations. The officers and men of 1 Division remained resolute in what, at the start of the operation, appeared a desperate situation, yet they persisted and gave confidence to their colleagues in 29 Division. Without them, the invaders might never have got off OMAHA beach on D-Day.

The Price of Error

In retrospect it is important to examine to what extent factors other than the strength of the enemy in the assault area, and the heavy sea and high wind, contributed to the difficulties experienced at OMAHA.

It was a tactical decision to assault head-on the main enemy fortifications, which were known to be located so as to cover the re-entrants in the bluff. This was contrary to our (British) previous experience and training, which had always emphasized the advantage of landing *between* enemy strong-points in order to attack them from the flank or rear. The record shows, for example, that one unit of 130 US Rangers landed directly opposite the track leading to Vierville, and only half of them reached the base of the bluff; but just a few hundred yards to their right, 450 men of another Ranger battalion landed between the strong-points and suffered only five casualties before reaching the bottom of the slope.

It is also worth recording that the decision not to use flail (mine-clearing) tanks and specialist armoured engineers' tanks, deprived the troops of any specialist equipment with which to deal with pill-boxes, clear wire entanglements, place explosives on concrete barriers, or lift mines. Even as late as the afternoon, troops were crossing the shingle bank in single file because the clearance of mines by hand was taking such a long time.

Hobart's 'Funnies'

Colonel (later, General Sir) Percy Hobart was one of the great pre-war prophets of the future importance of armoured fighting vehicles. At the outbreak of war he was placed in charge of the development of a series of specialised tanks, four of which, all used in the Normandy invasion, are illustrated here. Fascine tanks carried bundles of palings which, placed in shell holes or against walls, enabled tanks to cross over these obstructions. Carpet-layers carried a roll of heavy canvas track that could be laid over soft clay areas. Flail tanks thrashed the ground to explode land mines and the Amphibious (DD) tank, had sufficient buoyancy to make its way to shore unaided.

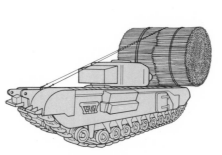

Fascine tank

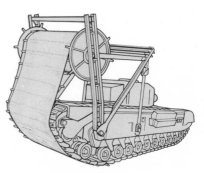

Carpet-layer tank

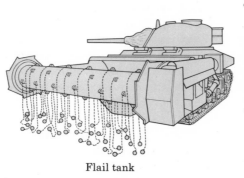

Flail tank

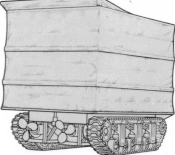

Amphibious tank

Embarkation (right)
One Sherman 'Crab' flail tank and two fascine tanks are loaded on to a landing barge in readiness for the invasion of Normandy. From the same design team came the Bridge-layer tank and the Flame-thrower – one of the most terrifying weapons of the war and one used to devastating effect in Holland where it was used against troops manning trenches and dugout positions at the far side of high-banked canals.

In action (left)
A flail tank of 79 Armoured Division photographed in action on the D-Day beaches.

The Eastern Sector Assault

In the Eastern (British) Task Force sector, the three assaulting divisions went ashore in adjacent sectors along the 25 miles of coast between Port-en-Bessin and the River Orne. The terrain was open and the ground sloped gently inland, and – as at UTAH and OMAHA – the landing areas allocated to the assault divisions were each about one mile in width.

The pattern of D-Day operations inevitably differed from that which prevailed on the American sector. At UTAH General Collins had to consider not only his main task northwards to capture Cherbourg but also how to link up with 82 Airborne Division, the main part of which had captured Ste-Mère-Eglise to the east of the landing area, and with 101 Airborne Division, of which the HQ and elements of two brigades were at Hiesville to the south. Account also had to be taken of the airborne groups fighting stoutly, but without co-ordination, over a very wide area. They could not immediately be concentrated in readiness for a thrust westwards across the River Merderet to the west coast of the peninsula to isolate Cherbourg, or for a drive southwards to Carentan as a preliminary to linking up with the OMAHA forces. To this divided situation was added the problem of resisting German counter-attacks, because the enemy were so confused by the dispersion of the airborne contingents that it was almost impossible to predict from which direction any counter-attack might come.

Throughout the British sector the enemy defence system that had to be penetrated was relatively uniform and can therefore more readily be described, since the terrain demanded no special variations from one beach to another.

As elsewhere there were three lines of underwater obstacles – most of them fitted with explosive charges – the outer line of piles sloping seaward to impale incoming craft. (After the assault, more than 2,500 obstacles of various types were counted on three and a quarter miles of GOLD beach.) The immediate coast defences were sited 300 to 400 yards from the normal high-tide line, and included armoured concrete strong-points enclosing heavily wired and mined gun emplacements. Between them and the shore, in areas where there were sand dunes, the minefield was six rows deep. In other areas there were concrete sea walls sometimes up to 12 feet high, with concrete machine-gun posts sited above them. The heavier 155mm gun batteries were usually about 1,200 yards from the beach, some in concrete casemates, others on mobile mountings. Overall in the forward area there was a bewildering dispersion of minefields and obstacles laid in lines diagonal to, rather than parallel to, the coastline.

It is difficult to give an exact definition of the density of fire-power behind the beaches, but in one area, probably typical of all areas of the American and British sectors, air photographs revealed

Hidden menace
The barrel of a heavy artillery piece protrudes from beneath its camouflage cover at the head of one of the eastern sector landing beaches.

on a 25-mile coastal stretch: 124 D.P. (Dual Purpose) 88mm guns; 27 batteries of 75mm and 155mm guns; 21 heavy A.A. pieces, and some 500 fixed position mortars and heavy machine-guns.

The Eastern Task Force naval commander was Rear Admiral Sir Philip Vian RN. Commanding Second Army was Lieut.-General Sir Miles Dempsey, to whom Montgomery gave as his first task the rapid establishment of a secure bridgehead of sufficient depth inland, 'to protect the flank of First US Army while the latter captures Cherbourg and the Brittany ports'.

The seaborne assault was made by three divisions: 50 Infantry Division on GOLD beach, under 30 Corps commanded by Lieut.-General G. C. Bucknall; and 3 Canadian Division on JUNO and 3 British Division on SWORD, both under 1 Corps commanded by Lieut.-General J. Crocker. (Lieut.-General Bucknall was succeeded as commander of 30 Corps on 4 August by Lieut.-General Brian Horrocks.)

[For simplicity, in this account the terms GOLD beach, JUNO beach, and so on, are used to describe the landing areas, although the codenames GOLD, JUNO, etc., were actually designated 'Assault Areas' and were further subdivided into individual 'Landing Beaches'. Thus; GOLD Area comprised 'Jig' and 'King' beaches; OMAHA Area comprised 'Dog', 'Easy' and 'Fox' beaches, and so on.]

GOLD Beach

50 Division attacked on a two-brigade front together with 47 Commando. The right-hand brigade was to clear le Hamel and thrust westwards along the coast through Arromanches to Port-en-Bessin, in order to meet up with 5 US Corps. 47 Commando was to capture Port-en-Bessin by encirclement, while the region east of the town was threatened by the main body. The other brigade was ordered to cordon off la Rivière and strike south, directly towards St-Léger on the Bayeux–Caen road, which stood on a dominant feature. The gap between the centre-lines of the leading brigades was to be filled by the two reserve brigades: these were to begin landing at 1000 hours and their orders were to make a rapid thrust to Bayeux, and the high ground south of the town.

H-hour on GOLD was scheduled for 0725 hours, because the British Command had opted for approximately two hours of naval bombardment prior to the landings. This proved a wise decision.

The map shows the type and distribution of beach defence installations on 'King' beach in the GOLD Assault Area as known to Allied intelligence in the weeks before D-Day.

German beach defences

Light machine gun	
AA machine gun	
Mobile gun – light	
Medium	
A/tk	
Open enplacement	
Gun casemate	
75mm, 155mm guns –	
In open emplacement	
In concrete	
Concrete artillery O.P.	
Wireless station	
Communication trench	
Dug-out shelter	
Concrete shelter	
Hutted camp	
Steel Hedgehogs	XXX
A/tk ditch	
Barbed wire obstacle	
Single fence	
Mines	
Dump	
Under construction	
Constructional activity	
Unconfirmed	
Unspecified infantry weapon	

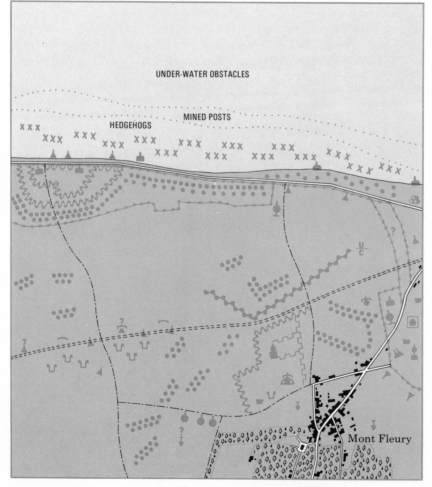

UNDER-WATER OBSTACLES

MINED POSTS

HEDGEHOGS

Mont Fleury

Although the air bombing of the enemy defences had been accurate, a German six-inch battery at Longues, west of Arromanches, had survived due to the extra casemates ordered by Rommel. This battery opened up on the ships approaching the coast, but within 20 minutes, the British cruiser HMS *Ajax* had silenced the enemy guns. It is interesting to note that although the casemates of one of the German guns did not receive a direct hit from the cruiser's guns, the high-explosive shells blew in part of the foundations, which had the effect of putting out of action the sighting gear and radar unit, rendering the gun useless.

The assembly of the landing craft which, in the case of the Eastern Task Force, was seven miles offshore, proved extremely difficult, with seas running even higher than had been experienced at OMAHA. Some craft were delayed by flooded engine rooms, and vehicle ferries were constantly breaking their towropes. It was too rough to launch the amphibious tanks, due at the beach ahead of the infantry, and they had to be taken to the shore in the craft carrying

Beach organization
Men of the 13th/18th Hussars assemble on the beach as hundreds more men pour from the landing craft grounded in the shallows. Red Cross men can be seen helping the wounded ashore and tending those hit by enemy fire from the beach-head.

them. The timing schedule was further upset by the tide, which was driven in-shore by the wind some 30 minutes earlier than normal.

The infantry, packed together in their violently tossing craft, had been given anti-seasickness pills, but they were not effective in such seas and most of the men arrived on the beach weak from vomiting, and thoroughly wet and cold; but such was the skill of the crews that the craft hit their beaching positions with very few casualties. The marshalling operation had been quickly rearranged so that the tank-carrying craft were first in, and had started engaging the enemy positions by the time the infantry waded ashore. The beach clearance armoured vehicles were, however, late and it was soon found that the stronghold of le Hamel was so heavily protected that it had survived all prior attempts to level it. It was fortunate indeed that tanks were ashore to cover the troops and to aid their attack, and that the flail tanks and engineer tanks were not far behind. Three of the four flails which make for le Hamel were hit and set on fire, but the fourth charged on through the village, and by some exceptional good fortune continued exploding mines and firing its 75mm gun long enough to provide a diversion for half an infantry battalion to rush across the foreshore and get behind the enemy fire positions – which had limited traverse in their casemates. The adventurous tank was, alas, finally blown up, but the courage and tenacity of its crew had enabled the infantry to reach Asnelles, a village south of le Hamel. It was some time before the stronghold itself was finally overcome.

The other battalion on the right sector of the beach was out of range of the le Hamel guns, and made rapid progress. In spite of the high seas and wind, for once the beach clearance went according to plan. The carpet tanks laid tracks for vehicles over some clay patches in the sand; flails exploded the mines and did a double turn by assisting the infantry with covering fire, while engineer tanks smashed concrete obstacles. This clearance team had provided three exits from the beach in just over an hour, and the infantry were soon on their way westwards: destination, Port-en-Bessin. Unfortunately, however, they found Arromanches strongly held by tough 352 Division troops, and only after a planned armoured and infantry attack in the afternoon was the small town cleared and the Germans forced to withdraw to the next village, Tracy-sur-Mer.

The German defences facing the eastern half of the 50 Division landing beach had not escaped the preparatory bombing, and most of la Rivière village was in ruins. But one heavily protected stronghold remained, and the troops racing ashore to find cover were subjected to sustained machine-gun fire, and an 88mm gun brewed up two engineer beach clearance tanks. But a flail tank, taking advantage of the enemy's limited power of traverse, moved in from the flank and fired a belt of 'Besa' through the embrasure at point-blank range. (On the Sherman tank there was mounted coaxially with the 75mm gun a BESA machine-gun.)

The stronghold gave up, but there followed some street fighting in the village. Meanwhile our troops west of la Rivière penetrated the German defences more readily. In their engagement with the enemy, great credit must be given to the special armoured clearance tanks manned by the Royal Engineers, 6 Assault Regiment. A party of three of these tanks moved against a pillbox and its adjoining wall, from which the enemy were firing automatic weapons and hurling grenades. The pillbox was shattered by petard (blockbuster explosive) and the tanks broached the wall – and unsuspectedly dropped four feet on to a roadway behind. The German soldiers were more surprised than the bruised tank crews, and proceeded to withdraw smartly. The British pushed on to the Meuvaines ridge.

Tank casualty
A Sherman flail tank of 79th Armoured Division lies stranded on the beach with its right-side track wrecked by a direct hit.

Battle scars
One of the huge German guns lies silent – its concrete emplacement scarred by Allied shells.

Difficult vehicle
One of the amphibious Duplex Drive Shermans makes its way ashore at Jig Green beach on 7 June. The tanks were difficult to control and many were lost in the rough seas on D-Day. Here the driver has reached the beach safely but his vehicle is slewing sideways as the tracks churn the sand in the surf zone.

The momentum of the attack was restored with the arrival of the follow-up brigades in the middle of the day. They were late due to difficulties in the rough seas, but once ashore were able to advance without the beach clearance problems which had bedevilled OMAHA and, to a much lesser extent, the le Hamel landings. Channels had been cleared through the underwater obstacles, and a number of exits, free of mines and obstacles, were prepared from the beach to the interior.

The defences at le Hamel proved truly formidable however and the 352 Division garrison fought as gallantly here as in its other sectors. Bearing in mind that they were cut off, with no hope of reinforcements and no chance of making a withdrawal, they stood their ground literally to the last man.

The units of 50 British Division, supported by fire from the destroyers offshore, maintained their progress and by 2100 hours, although by this time very tired, had overrun two miles of fortified coast and captured the town of Arromanches and the neighbouring cliff-tops. This advance had particular significance, because it cleared the way for the engineers to begin assembling the Mulberry harbour off Arromanches as planned, and the towing of components across the Channel from England could now start.

During these engagements the most important task of 30 British Corps – the capture of Bayeux – was being undertaken by the two reserve brigades, purposely landed after the leading formations had cleared the beaches and were occupying the attention of the forward German defences. By evening one brigade was outside the town on the north side, having advanced six miles, and patrols sent into the town reported only German stragglers there – the main garrison having withdrawn to the south. Effectively Bayeux was captured, though the troops did not occupy it in the darkness. But equally importantly the main lateral route from Caen to the west had been denied to the enemy, so that he could not use it to send reinforcements to the critical OMAHA sector. In fact, the Germans were at this point sending reinforcements from the west towards Bayeux. East of Bayeux, the brigade that intended to establish itself at St-Léger halted for the night just north of the Caen–Bayeux road. It had fought and marched six miles.

Although all three Eastern Task Force divisions had the benefit of previous battle experience, 50 Division had had the longest and most varied fighting record, having seen service in the North African desert, and later in the Sicily and southern Italy invasions, and in some measure this accounts for its steady endurance on D-Day. It was the only Allied division to reach its objectives on that day, and this reflection leads to increasing admiration of the American divisions at UTAH and OMAHA who, with the sole exception of 1 US Division, had to undergo their 'baptism of fire' in the most difficult and in all respects dangerous operation in war – a seaborne assault. When this is taken into account, what the Americans achieved on D-Day is all the more remarkable.

In considering 1 British Corps' operations, it must be noted that on the west flank of 50 Division there remained a gap of some six or seven miles of German-held coastline separating 30 Corps from 5 US Corps at OMAHA: 47 British Commando was within sight of Port-en-Bessin, after a fighting advance of no less than nine miles, but the town had yet to be cleared of enemy; and on the east flank, 50 Division had made firm contact with the neighbouring 3 Canadian Division on JUNO beach.

The three assault formations of 1 British Corps – 3 Canadian, 3 British and 6 Airborne Divisions – had what proved to be the most formidable and exacting of all the D-Day tasks.

In simplest terms, 6 Airborne was to create a bridgehead east of the parallel Caen canal and River Orne, and ensure the seizing and guarding of the bridges on the only lateral road between Caen and the sea which linked the proposed bridgehead with the seaborne forces landing to the west. The bridgehead, though necessarily restricted in size until it was possible to reinforce it, was essential for the possible strategic and tactical manoeuvres which might later prove necessary in the capturing of Caen, or the development of thrusts to the east or southeast of the River Orne.

3 British Division was given the task of capturing Caen, over eight miles from the landing areas and in the most exposed and heavily defended area of the assault front. Caen was the most vital strategic communications centre on the invasion frontage, and the only German reserve Panzer division close to the beaches, the 21, was known to be in the area between Caen and Falaise some 20 miles away on a direct main road. Even before 1 Corps started landing, it was already known that elements of 21 Panzer Division were moving against 6 Airborne Division.

Finally, 3 Canadian Division was required to attempt the deepest D-Day penetration inland, 11 miles, to reach and capture Carpiquet airfield, immediately west of Caen.

JUNO Beach

On the right of 1 Corps' assault, 3 Canadian Division landed in the JUNO sector. The landing beach was astride the River Seulles, and had caused misgivings during the planning because of the outcrop of reefs offshore. To ensure that the tide would be high enough for the landing craft to clear them, H-hour was delayed 15 minutes to 0735. This incurred a risk, because it meant that the tide would be that much higher up the beach, and the disembarkation points would be in the middle of the belts of underwater obstacles. In the event, since the rough sea and wind conditions on JUNO turned out to be worse than any encountered elsewhere on D-Day, the landing craft were delayed in taking up station at the lowering position, and arrived up to 25 minutes late (around 0800 hours). The result of the delay was that the higher tide carried the craft right through the heavily mined obstacle complex before they beached. Remarkably enough, very few craft were sunk or damaged on the run-in, but when after discharging their loads they attempted to withdraw out to sea, the losses were appalling: of one batch of 24 craft, only four returned safely to their 'mother ship'.

As in the American sector the Canadian infantry arrived at the beaches ahead of their tanks, only to find that the German beach defences were virtually intact. Owing to cloud conditions above and bad visibility at ground level, the bombing and shelling had over-reached the strongholds and, by now fully aware of what was happening on their flanks, the defenders were ready for battle, having largely recovered from the shock of the heavy bombing behind them.

The attack was launched on a two-brigade front. On the west, some amphibious tanks had been launched a few hundred yards off-shore, and were soon supporting the infantry. But the craft of the engineer beach clearance tanks did not cope so readily with the heavy seas, and did not arrive until about 0830. Although the infantry, with outstanding courage, managed to overcome the enemy positions sited on the waterfront, the problem – as we have seen on some other beaches – was to clear exits from the beach to the interior.

By mid-morning, two battalions had made about two miles of progress, but the beaches were choked with transport, stores, guns and armoured vehicles, and in the frustration this caused, the momentum of the operation rapidly faded.

On the east side of the landing, the brigade suffered very much from the same adverse conditions; the amphibious D.D. tanks could not be launched in the heavy swell and had to be brought in by the craft carrying them, while the tide, surging inshore before the wind, brought the infantry craft to within 100 yards of the defence wall which ran along the back of the beach. The stronghold at Bernières-sur-Mer, to the left, was in full action and, deprived of tanks or any other form of immediate support, the troops emerging from the surf

Guiding light
Sherman tanks of 13/18th Hussars (27th Beach Brigade) edge their way cautiously through the minefield of underwater obstacles, guided toward their landing beaches by colour-coded flares.

in full view of the enemy had no recourse but to make a desperate dash across the 100-yard gap to seek shelter at the foot of the wall from the murderous short-range small-arms fire. To give just one example, one of the assault companies, consisting of some 110 men, lost one-half its strength in that short dash. Such was the seriousness of the situation that on the personal initiative of the captain and the senior army officer aboard, a craft carrying an anti-aircraft gun fitted to fire at sea, came close inshore and poured continuous fire on the front and west side of the Bernières strong-point, using high-velocity 4.7-inch shrapnel shells. I believe the craft ran aground in making this gallant gesture, but happily it was recovered intact.

The Canadians were not to be discouraged by such an unpropitious start, and they had already cleared a way for the follow-up French-Canadian regiment (de la Chaudière) to move through Bernières. But they soon became held by gunfire from Bény-sur-Mer about three miles to the south, a position which resisted capture for some two hours. Meanwhile, the reserve brigade had landed, and a traffic pile-up in Bernières and back to the beach took nearly three hours to sort out. Valuable time lost could not be regained: though the front units had, by nightfall, covered seven miles, they were still four miles from Carpiquet airfield. It was infuriating to all concerned that it was not so much the enemy which had held them back, nor physical tiredness, nor lack of drive and confidence: it was the chaotic congestion at the back which, with more imaginative planning, might have been avoided. The unhappy fact is that a half-squadron of Canadian tanks actually reached the Caen–Bayeux road at Bretteville; there was no enemy opposition, so they advanced down the road towards Caen almost to Carpiquet, hoping to find other Canadians in the area. Had the route for armour, guns and reinforcements been kept open at Bernières, instead of holding up the operation for three hours, there appeared little opposition which could have stopped 9 Canadian Brigade from reaching Carpiquet, where the stray tanks from Bretteville would have joined them.

If 1 Corps had been able to become established at Carpiquet, the whole story of the subsequent battle for Caen would have been rewritten: more immediately, had the Canadians reached Carpiquet on D-Day, it would have added a further distraction to the movement of 21 Panzer Division, and enabled 3 British Division to get beyond Biéville-sur-Orne, which was barely three miles from the outskirts of Caen.

As it was, the isolated tanks had to withdraw to Camilly for replenishment, since they had not been followed up, and it was left to observe that 9 Canadian Brigade, in spite of all disappointments, had penetrated farther inland than any other Allied formation. Moreover, the link-up with 50 British Division had at last been made at la Rivière.

SWORD Beach

3 British Division, in the SWORD sector, assaulted on a one-brigade front. The landing beach selected was to the east of Lion-sur-Mer. The orders were that the division should make straight for Caen and seize a bridgehead there over the River Orne; the first objective was the feature near Périers-sur-le-Dan, which the leading brigade was to hold, while the follow-up formations passed through, on the line of the road to Caen.

H-hour was at 0725 and the first-wave craft arrived on time, preceded by the strongest and most effective air and warship bombardment on any of the D-Day beaches. In spite of heavy seas and bad visibility, 21 out of 25 launched amphibious tanks landed, together with the engineer clearance-team tanks, ahead of the infantry. The clearance of the foreshore presented no great problems, but along the sand dunes behind lay a maze of fortifications, obstacles and mines. Thanks to the timely arrival of the tanks and engineers, by 0930 the assault brigade had captured Hermanville-sur-Mer, about a mile and a half inland. Here, however, they found the Périers feature held by infantry and 88mm guns of 21 German Panzer Division. The 88mm gun line obliged the British tanks to fall back, and the infantry battalions went to ground.

Back at the beach, the left-hand-sector battalion had first to attack and neutralize a series of strong-points, and freedom from machine-gun fire was only achieved when 4 British Commando broke into the west side of the small town of Ouistreham.

The onshore wind drove the tide in so fast that the engineers had insufficient time to clear all the underwater obstacles before the follow-up wave arrived, and great skill was needed to bring the craft in safely. And on SWORD beach and its exits, there followed traffic congestion as experienced elsewhere; indeed the (third) reserve brigade had to be held back, and did not get to the shore until mid-afternoon.

Brief respite
Shattered remains of a once-fine building show the violence of the battle for the beaches. During a lull in the fighting for Hermanville sur Mer, men of the 13/18 Hussars erect shelters and establish communication with other units.

The record of 3 British Division is the most disappointing of all the assault sectors. Having started off with commendable *élan*, with the rapid capture of Hermanville, the progress of the division afterwards gave the impression of overcautiousness. It was stated earlier that all three British assault divisions had had previous battle experience, but perhaps it should be added that 3 Division had not previously taken part in a seaborne invasion assault. A more dynamic formation would not have dug in at Hermanville, but would have devised a plan, with the tanks, supporting artillery and tactical air force, designed to outflank the enemy at Périers. This should not be taken as criticism of the troops but rather a comment on the lack of training and battle experience of some of their officers.

The attack on Colleville took longer perhaps than would have been expected, for the enemy troops in the village were from 716 German Division – coastal defence troops who were spread over a wide area from north of Bretteville right across to the area east of 6 Airborne Division. The whole sector in which 3 Division was operating had been saturated with sustained fire by aircraft and warships, and apart from a Panzer Grenadier battalion on the west side of the Caen canal (belonging to 21 Panzer Division, which was attacking 6 British Airborne holding the Bénouville bridge), there was no concentrated enemy force to impede the British advance. Indeed 1 British Special Service Brigade, led by its commander playing the bagpipes, marched straight through Ouistreham to the River Orne, where an engineer bridging party got the troops across the canal and river to link up at 1330 hours with 6 Airborne Division. The brigade then started to fight its way towards the coastal battery at Merville, still held by British airborne troops facing German troops in Franceville-Plage.

Regrettably it was not until towards the end of the day that 3 Division finally relieved 6 Airborne Division at the Bénouville bridge, and meanwhile the foremost troops of the division were still on the line Biéville–Blainville, three miles from the outskirts of Caen. The division had made few calls on the air forces for direct support, which was of course a mistake, but the air cover had rendered a valuable contribution to 3 Division's operations since there had been no intervention by the main tank force of 21 Panzer Division during D-Day. The battle groups of Panzer Grenadiers had, since the early hours of D-Day, made repeated counter-attacks against 6 British Airborne Division, on both sides of the Orne. These had all been repulsed. We now know that tank groups had been destined to reinforce the efforts against 6 Airborne, but when the seaborne landings became known, the Commander of 21 Panzer recalled them and ordered that they should cross the Orne at Caen and at Colombelles to concentrate on the north side of the city. Any movement of these tanks observed from the air at once received the attention of the tactical air force. At General Dempsey's request on the morning of D-Day, all German troop movements in the vicinity of Caen were subjected to almost continuous air attack.

Maj.-General Feuchtinger, the commander of 21 Panzer Division, claimed that from the southwest side of Caen his armoured regiment – reduced by air attacks and breakdowns to 90 serviceable tanks – together with two infantry battalions, advanced northwards to oppose the Allies. It was not until 1600 hours that British tanks of the Staffordshire Yeomanry, scouting south of Biéville, reported German tanks advancing northwards.

About 40 enemy tanks put in a 'cavalry charge' attack, apparently not expecting the quickly established gun line comprising a squadron of the Staffordshire Yeomanry tanks, some 17-pounder self-propelled (S.P.) anti-tank guns of 20 Anti-Tank Regiment R.A. together with the 6-pounder anti-tank guns of the Shropshire Light Infantry. Four leading German tanks were brewed up and the enemy swung away into the cover of some neighbouring woods. They were pursued by the Yeomanry and artillery fire and suffered further casualties, whereupon they made a wide detour to the east and came in again towards the Périers ridge. A squadron of the Staffordshire tanks was awaiting them 'hull down' by Trig. Point 61, and at least 13 were knocked out: the German tanks again withdrew. Feuchtinger stated after the war that he had started the day with 124 tanks, and that by nightfall he had only 70 runners left. This seems an exaggeration: our troops counted 20 abandoned tanks and the RAF knocked out six in a Typhoon aircraft rocket attack on the outskirts of Caen. There is no record of the successes achieved by the RAF in the other rocket attacks they had made.

The Shropshires made a further sortie southwards from Biéville along the Caen road, but found that there was a strong enemy force astride the highway at Lebisey: it was growing dark, and because of

Typhoon attack
The two photographs on the facing page show the devastating effect of rocket-firing Typhoon aircraft when used against armour and supply columns.

the danger of a renewed attack on their exposed right flank they returned to Biéville for the night. Almost at last light, patrols of another British battalion near the Bénouville bridge defences found that there was an apparently isolated German detachment near a locality called le Port. The British were mounting an attack, although it was already nearly 2100 hours, when the roar of aircraft engines above heralded the passage at low altitude of two columns of Allied transport aircraft towing gliders, strongly escorted by fighters above them. 6 Airborne Division, without much of its heavy equipment, had had little enough assistance during the day, but had fought off numerous counter-attacks – the most determined and dangerous of which were made by the Panzer Grenadier battalions. 1 SAS Brigade had arrived in the afternoon and three Commando units had reinforced them. But now, at last, the remainder of the Airborne Division had arrived, virtually doubling the fighting strength of the formation. In addition to two strong battalions, the glider convoy included the armoured reconnaissance unit, some light artillery, anti-tank guns and a medical unit. Six hundred containers of stores and ammunition were also dropped by parachute.

The arrival was fortuitous. The German Seventh Army telephone records include a report that states, 'Attack by 21 Panzer Division rendered useless by heavy concentration of airborne troops,' and the report which was sent to Rommel was in similar terms. We knew in due course, from radio intercepts, that 21 Panzer Division, less the battalions east of the Orne, had been ordered to withdraw to a line running eastwards from Cambes-en-Plaine to the Caen canal.

It was nearly midnight when the Royal Warwickshire Battalion, having cleared le Port, took over the Bénouville bridge from the splendid airborne party which had held out there since the early hours of the morning.

Before summing up the position at the end of D-Day, mention must be made of the German plans for dealing with the developing situation which was now of increasing concern to Hitler, and to his senior commanders Von Rundstedt and Rommel. After Rommel's pleading before D-Day, and Von Rundstedt's urgent requests in the early hours of D-Day, Hitler at last released both 12SS Panzer Division (which he had allowed to move forward from Lisieux, but not to be committed) and Panzer Lehr Division to Von Rundstedt. News of Hitler's decision, made at 1400 hours, reached Seventh Army HQ at 1600. 12SS had been observed by Allied air reconnaissance to be on the move during D-Day, but because it was vulnerable to rocket attacks from Typhoon aircraft, the commander sent his tanks forward in batches between wooded hide-outs so that progress in daylight was very slow. It had become clear, however, that 12SS was making for Caen, but that it could not reach the battle on D-Day though it could be expected on D + 1. Panzer Lehr had to start off from the area of Chartres, and it remained to be seen what rate of progress it would achieve in the face of Allied air attacks.

Airborne support
Halifaxes and Hamilcar gliders of 6th Airborne Division flying in over the beach-heads to bring much needed reinforcement to the paratroops dropped during the night of 5/6 June.

Litter of war
An R.A.F. reconnaissance photograph shows a sea of discarded parachutes in the fields northeast of Caen. The British 'Horsa' glider would have carried the paras' heavier equipment including artillery pieces, light vehicles and anti-tank weapons.

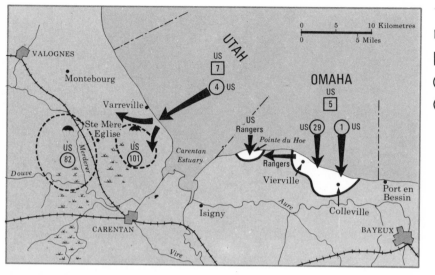

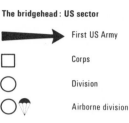

The bridgehead : US sector

➤ First US Army

☐ Corps

○ Division

○▽ Airborne division

REFLECTIONS AT THE END OF D-DAY

Winston Churchill described the assault on Normandy as 'the most difficult and complicated operation that has ever taken place'. Because of the changing technology and weaponry of warfare, no action of its kind may ever take place again. Yet there are lessons to be learnt from it, which for all time will influence the study of war.

There is no doubt that the most important single factor in the success of the invasion was the mastery in the air established by the Allied air forces before D-Day, and subsequently maintained throughout the operation. This dominant air supremacy had an adverse effect on every aspect of the Germans' defence philosophy, planning, conduct of operations and logistical capability. Strategic bombing of oil installations and industrial plants affected the enemy's sources of essential equipment and vehicle fuel. Allied air power had played the major part in the campaign against U-boats; it had protected the UK invasion bases from bombing attacks; it had obstructed Luftwaffe air reconnaissance to the extent that the assembly and Channel crossing of the massive armada of ships and craft had not only been unmolested but took place unnoticed until its arrival in daylight off the French coast; it had been an important element in the pre-D-Day Deception Plan, and had provided the vitally effective radar deception plan during the night of D—1. Its interdiction programme had immobilized the railways in the essential areas, and destroyed the bridges on the lower Seine and the Loire. It was only in the bombing of beach defences during the pre-assault stage that results were largely disappointing, due to the incidence of cloud and bad visibility, though where conditions were favourable, as at UTAH, the air attacks proved highly successful.

The bridgehead: British sector

→ Second British Army

☐ Corps

○ Division

○ Airborne Division

○ Armoured Division

Throughout D-Day, in addition to the maintenance of air cover over the Channel and the combat area, tactical air forces were engaged in supporting the ground troops throughout the daylight hours. British 2 Tactical Air Force logged over 100 attacks. Long-range fighters of 8 US Air Force, normally used to escort the heavy bombers, were active in attacking ground targets over a wide area of the battle in the south and east regions, and 9 US Air Force employed over 2,700 aircraft for similar attacks in the Cherbourg Peninsula, and in areas to the south and southwest of OMAHA. 8 US Air Force also provided 600 heavy bombers for attacks on nodal communication towns through which enemy reinforcements and supply columns were likely to pass, from St-Lô in the west to the area near Lisieux in the east.

The Luftwaffe was a spent force, and throughout the day our men on the ground, or afloat at sea, saw no sign of enemy aircraft. In fact, the enemy did make 36 sorties over the British sectors; only 12 of the aircraft showed fight, of which seven were shot down and the remainder turned back. The 9 US Air Force claimed five enemy aircraft shot down, presumably in the Cherbourg Peninsula sector. Just before last light, four Heinkel bombers scattered some bombs near the JUNO beach, but the aircraft were all shot down by a squadron of RAF Spitfires. It is thus difficult to account for the German claim to have made 319 sorties on D-Day with the loss of 31 aircraft destroyed and 16 damaged.

In air operations on the night of D−1 and on D-Day, Allied aircraft of all types had flown no less than 14,000 sorties, and suffered relatively light casualties: 127 aircraft were lost, and 63 were damaged but managed to return to base.

The preparations made by the Allied navies for the assault reached a climax on D-Day, when 130,000 men, with their vehicles and stores, were landed on the French coast. At this time the total number of naval personnel involved in the warships, landing ships, craft and barges was 112,800 British, 53,000 American and 5,000 of other Allied navies; in addition there were some 25,000 merchant navy seamen manning the transport vessels, making an overall total of approximately 196,000.

The accomplishment of putting the armies ashore in such adverse sea and wind conditions, without interference by German naval forces, was a remarkable achievement.

The distribution of the personnel landed was approximately:

GOLD	25,000	
JUNO	21,500	Total British and Canadians: 75,000
SWORD	29,000	Total American: 57,500
UTAH	23,250	
OMAHA	34,250	

The numbers of personnel were of the order of magnitude planned beforehand, but there was a short-fall in vehicles and stores. Taking only the British sector as an example, since comparable figures are not available for the US sector, the number of vehicles landed was 6,000, including 950 tanks and armoured vehicles (out of 1,050 planned), 240 field guns, and 280 anti-tank guns; altogether about 60 per cent of planned deliveries. The total of 4,000 tons of stores unloaded was about 75 per cent of the target. The main shortage was in medium artillery (which was greatly missed by the assault forces) and A.A. artillery, which fortunately was not in demand, given the absence of the Luftwaffe.

Bringing the craft ashore, and returning from the landing beach after unloading, in the heavy swell and gusty wind, demanded not only skill but also an element of good fortune, because of the underwater obstacles which, in varying degrees, were a problem on all beaches. The magnitude of the clearance task can be understood from a typical example: there were counted afterwards, on a typical run of three and a quarter miles of coastline, 2,500 obstacles, set in three lines. It was calculated that they weighed 900 tons in all and nearly all had fused mines or large shells attached. It is therefore remarkable that on the British sector no more than 258 craft were lost. The figure on the US sector was higher.

The naval anchorage defence was based on a cordon of minesweepers stationed at half-mile intervals, ready in particular to deal with mines dropped from aircraft. There were also roving patrols of destroyers and motor torpedo boats (MTBs) in the Channel, watching for surface craft encroachment. The system included, of course, fighter aircraft cover by day, and up to six squadrons of RAF Mosquitoes by night.

The incalculable importance of the fire support afforded to the ground troops by the Allied navies throughout the operation has seldom been adequately emphasised. After the prearranged naval bombardment before H-hour, during which, in the British Sector

D-Day Panorama
This U.S. Coast Guard photograph of part of the Western Task Force sector gives some idea of the enormity of the operation launched by the Allies at dawn on 6 June 1944.

alone, more than 30,000 shells (four-inch and larger) were poured into the coast defences by the destroyers and other close-support ships, the warships engaged the innumerable strongholds and defensive positions which had survived the preparatory air bombing raids. During the assault phase, a German Seventh Army report recorded that 'counter-attacks, successful at first, later suffered unusually high casualties in the neighbourhood of the coast through enemy naval gunfire'. More significant in this context is a report which Von Rundstedt sent to Hitler personally. He wrote: 'The guns of enemy warships have so powerful an effect on areas within their range that any advance into the zone dominated by fire from the sea is impossible. . . .'

The inevitable price
Although lower than many had predicted, Allied casualties at the end of D-Day were still in the order of 10,000 killed, wounded and missing; and of a total of some 6,000 American casualties, about half had been suffered at OMAHA. However, Montgomery was later to reflect that never before had any army been served so swiftly or so well by front-line medical teams.

In the first days of the invasion, fire support was provided by all types of naval vessels, from battleships to gun-carrying craft. As the fighting moved inland, the bombardment forces were reduced, but there remained at all times an average of two battleships or monitors, several cruisers and some destroyers in readiness for calls from the armies ashore.

At the end of D-Day, the Army had secured a foothold in Normandy. In spite of all the preparations that the Germans had made during the previous two years, including the elaborate systems designed to give timely warning of any seaborne attack, the Allies had achieved complete surprise. The Atlantic Wall had been breached at all the landing areas, and the coastal defences between them had already been cleared by the end of D-Day on much of the total assault frontage. The losses sustained by the Allies on D-Day were far less than had been feared. Among seaborne troops the British and Canadian casualties were about 4,200 (killed, wounded and missing): the total American casualties were about 6,000. Of the latter, some 3,000 were incurred at OMAHA. A later estimate of the total number of Allied men killed on D-Day itself was 2,500.

Fortunately, many of the 'missing' were able eventually to rejoin their units; this applies particularly to the airborne troops. The medical arrangements to provide rapid attention to the wounded were extremely well organized. Serious cases, able to travel, were evacuated to hospital in Britain by air, in the care of nursing sisters in the aircraft. It has been recorded that no army ever went overseas with such a comprehensive and skilled medical service as that provided for the Normandy invasion. Between 6 June and 31 August,

The life-line
No invading army could hope to hold its initial gains, far less penetrate inland, without constant replenishment. UTAH beach, on 12 June, is quiet and orderly as a steady stream of landing barges brings ashore men, vehicles, fuel, ammunition, food and medical supplies.

57,500 casualties were evacuated from France by sea and a further 22,500 by air.

But the intended objectives had not been reached, except for the evacuated town of Bayeux, which was not occupied until after dawn next morning. The main preoccupation of the Allied commanders was the situation at OMAHA, which remained highly vulnerable to a concentrated enemy counter-attack. The beach-heads had not yet been linked up into a continuous bridgehead; there remained gaps between UTAH and OMAHA, and from the east of OMAHA to 50 Division at Port-en-Bessin; and there was still a narrow enemy salient between JUNO and SWORD, embracing the very strongly organized enemy defensive system at Douvres.

Other immediate preoccupations were the uncertainty of the weather, and the fact that the overall build-up tables were already eight to 12 hours behind schedule.

On the other hand, the very favourable situation in the air gave cause for confidence, and in spite of the dispersion of the airborne divisions in the Cherbourg Peninsula and the presence there of two first-line German infantry divisions, 91 and 352, together with other reinforcements sent in May by Hitler's orders, there was every indication that operations were progressing well. This was important, for the capture of Cherbourg port was a high priority requirement, and also because the Allied front would not be 'tidy', and ready for the development of Montgomery's master plan, until the whole of First US Army was concentrated facing south, in a cordon across the base of the peninsula.

It was too early to appreciate the manner in which the enemy would react to the Allied landings. For Montgomery and Dempsey it was a surprise that 21 Panzer Division had taken so long to intervene in strength in the battle, and that the tank thrust made at last around 1600 hours had lacked tactical skill and been so readily repulsed. It was not known to the Allies that the division had experienced not only an exhausting day, having been alerted around 0130 hours, but also endless frustration at being 'pushed around'. To begin with, its commander, Feuchtinger, was not sure whether he was under command of the German 84 Corps, or under the newly formed HQ 47 Panzer Corps (along with 116 Panzer – on the Seine – and 2 Panzer located around Abbeville in the north), the commander of which had not yet been nominated; or under HQ Panzer Group West. However, Feuchtinger had standing orders that, in the event of an Allied landing, he was to send two battalion groups of Panzer Grenadiers with his anti-tank battalion to engage the enemy east of the River Orne. This he did, and their counter-attacks on 6 British Airborne Division have been mentioned earlier. His orders also specified that he should send his anti-aircraft unit to Caen, where it would join the Flak Command.

Time passed, and finally on his own personal initiative, presumably because his units on the Orne called for assistance, Feuchtinger sent a battle group including tanks to join the Panzer Grenadiers on the east side of the river. It was not until 0845 hours that a message was received placing 21 Panzer Division under 84 Corps. The commander, Marcks, told Feuchtinger that he wanted to send his division north and northwest of Caen, but that he was still awaiting permission to do so through the normal channels from OKW. At 1030 hours, Feuchtinger received his first clear order: he was to proceed north and northwest of Caen and restore the situation developing on the German front between Caen and Bayeux.

The battle group, which was on its way north, on the east side of the River Orne, had therefore to be diverted to the west side of Caen in order to link up with the main body, which was starting off from its location some 15 miles south of the city, near Falaise. These tank movements were quickly spotted by the Allied air forces, and were attacked repeatedly by the tactical air force and harassed by naval gunfire. A number of tanks were destroyed before the two columns of 21 Panzer Division were clear of Caen, by which time it was nearly 1500 hours. Their subsequent engagement with 3 British Division has already been described.

Though Montgomery was not to know it at the time, the muddled indecision of the German High Command in the handling of 21 Panzer Division on D-Day was fortuitous indeed. Had it been deployed in the morning, while 3 British Division were sorting out delays and congestion on the beaches, and while the reserve 9 Brigade was behind time and slow in its move inland, the whole SWORD beach landing might have been placed in jeopardy.

Awaiting orders
German tank crews stand idle in the villages and lanes south of Caen as Allied troops pour across the Normandy beaches. If these armoured divisions had been deployed swiftly and expertly, the D-Day landings would have come under serious threat.

PART V

The Allied Bridgehead

THE ESTABLISHMENT OF THE BRIDGEHEAD: 7–12 JUNE

General Montgomery's orders for D+1, to General Bradley commanding First US Army, were to complete the tasks necessary to set the scene for the capture of Cherbourg by 7 US Corps. In the south of the UTAH sector, the objectives were to capture the important road centre of Carentan, and to attack across the Taute-Vire canal towards Isigny-sur-Mer, to effect the link up with 5 US Corps. The Carentan estuary presented a difficult problem because of the Rivers Vire and Taute and the subsidiary complex of waterways and flooded areas associated with them. 7 US Corps had also to launch a thrust across the Cherbourg Peninsula to the west coast, in order to isolate Cherbourg. The Corps was, on 7–8 June, greatly assisted by the progressive concentration of the scattered groups of 82 and 101 Airborne Divisions, and by the arrival of 9 US Infantry Division.

The 5 US Corps at OMAHA had to consolidate its beach-head and link up on both flanks with its neighbouring formations. The magnificent manner in which 1 and 29 US Divisions, duly joined by 2 US Division, retrieved the critical situation in the sector will be evident later.

Second British Army was ordered to proceed with the capture of Caen, and to develop the bridgehead southwards across the Caen–Bayeux road. The narrow enemy salient, which included the enemy stronghold at Douvres, was to be eliminated so that 3 Canadian and 3 British Divisions could be firmly joined up.

Montgomery was anxious that the bridgehead should be continuous along the whole frontage, and to get it firmly established as quickly as possible. It was yet to be determined where the Germans would mount their major counter-attacks, but it was known that in addition to the arrival of 12SS Panzer Division south of Caen on the night of D-Day, other armoured divisions were on the move. Panzer Lehr, located near Chartres, and 2 Panzer, based near Amiens, were observed being loaded on to trains for transfer to the battle zones. In addition, 17SS Panzer Grenadier Division (which had no tanks) was preparing to leave Poitiers, south of the Loire.

In response to this intelligence, RAF Bomber Command attacked rail and road junctions on an arc from the south of the Cherbourg Peninsula to the area south of Paris, to delay the movement of reinforcements towards Normandy. By day, fighter-bombers delivered constant attacks on all movements observed on roads that converged on the Normandy area, and also created rubble and crater obstacles at key road centres.

UTAH Beach: 7 US Corps

101 US Airborne Division was concentrated in the southern sector of the beach-head in preparation for an advance on Carentan, which

Command post
Safely dug in beneath the crest of a bluff, one of the American assault units on UTAH beach takes a brief rest while radio contact is made with neighbouring units.

began on 9 June. The enemy 352 Division was meanwhile making determined efforts to prevent the junction between 7 and 5 US Corps, but by 10 June, 29 US Infantry Division had taken Isigny, and a bridge over the River Vire, and later on that day patrols from 29 Division made contact with 101 Airborne.

By 10 June, 5 US Corps had also joined up with 50 British Division near Port-en-Bessin and the enemy salient to Douvres, north of Caen, had at last been eliminated, so that when 101 Airborne Division captured Carentan, and the road Carentan–Isigny was cleared on 12 June, the Allied bridgehead was made continuous throughout the invasion frontage.

Meanwhile 4 US Division, having joined up with 82 US Airborne Division in Ste-Mère-Eglise on 7 June, struck north, and by 10 June was engaged in heavy fighting near Montebourg. 82 Airborne thrust westwards from St-Mère-Eglise, across the River Merderet, making for the west coast of the peninsula, but was staunchly resisted by the first-line 91 German Infantry Division.

OMAHA Beach: 5 US Corps

At first light on 7 June, the OMAHA beaches were still covered by directed fire from German artillery, and by some machine-gun positions on the flanks. Any attempt to move westwards was strongly contested, but to the east fighting patrols of 1 US Division made further contact with the British 47 Commando, which had captured Port-en-Bessin.

By 8 June, the American forces had got into their stride, and they advanced with tremendous *élan*. It has been noted that 29 US Division smashed the west flank of 352 German Division to capture Isigny and a bridge over the River Vire on 9 June. Firm contact was now made with 101 Airborne Division. On the east side, 1 US Division crossed the River Aure and linked up with 50 British Division west of Bayeux on 8 June, and then pushed south to secure the Forest of Cérisy and Balleroy on 10 June. All the available resources of the German 352 Division were at this time committed to resist the advance on Carentan. The other enemy reserves in the area had already been sent to the Bayeux sector, and in the centre of 5 US Corps' advance, 2 US Division made very rapid progress from the beach-head, and cut the road from Bayeux to St-Lô to the west of the Forest of Cérisy.

In spite of the flooded country and strong German resistance, 101 Airborne Division captured Carentan on 12 June, and were there joined by elements of 29 US Division.

GOLD Beach: 30 British Corps

On the morning of 7 June the deserted town of Bayeux was occupied and 50 Division, with 8 Armoured Brigade and, already arriving, 7 Armoured Division, was engaged in a thrust towards Tilly-sur-Seulles. The intention was to reach Villers-Bocage and thence secure a crossing over the River Odon in order to threaten the communications of enemy troops defending Caen. Although, on 11 June, 7 Armoured Division fought its way into Tilly, it was later driven back by a very strong counter-attack. The German 12SS Panzer Division and Panzer Lehr Division were now in action in the sector.

The villages on the line la-Belle-Epine–Tilly–Brouay were established German strongholds, which included anti-tank defences protected by infantry. General Dempsey therefore ordered a re-grouping, whereby 7 Armoured Division would switch to the right flank of 50 Division and drive towards Villers-Bocage from the west.

JUNO Beach and SWORD Beach: 1 British Corps

Operations for the capture of Caen were continued on D+1 by 3 Canadian Division from the northwest and west, and by 3 British Division from the north. The Canadians extended their front to the south of the Caen–Bayeux road, linking with 30 Corps troops in the Brouay area.

3 British Division launched attacks against Caen directly from the north, but little progress was made. 12SS Panzer and 21 Panzer Divisions with 716 Infantry Division were strongly posted covering the city.

East of the River Orne, the British were concerned in resisting persistent counter-attacks. It was obvious that the Germans intended to prevent the expansion of the bridgehead made by 6 Airborne Division, and that reinforcements were needed in that sector.

The Enemy Situation: 12 June

We now know that Hitler's reaction to the news of the Allied landings on 6 June was an order that the incursion should be annihilated by the evening of that day. He still persisted in the belief that the Allied operation in Normandy was a diversion – no more than a prelude to the main invasion which would come later in the Pas de Calais. The strength of the Allied landings and subsequent build-up was therefore grossly underestimated by the German High Command.

There appeared to be no co-ordinated German plan to deal with a major onslaught in Normandy, and the Allied offensive policy, together with the delays caused to the movement of German reserves by the Allied air forces, forced the enemy to resort to plugging the holes in his defensive deployment. Subsequently it seemed clear that Rommel had decided that the Allied intentions were primarily to capture Cherbourg, and also to take Rouen by a thrust from the east of Caen to the Seine – presumably with the prospect of moving north to join the anticipated main Allied assault forces in the Pas de Calais. Hence his plan was to destroy the Allied bridgehead on the east of the River Orne and, at the same time, to concentrate sufficient forces to prevent 7 US Corps from capturing the port of Cherbourg.

Owing to the remarkably successful air attacks on German troop movements, and to bad communications and shortage of vehicle fuel, Rommel was forced to commit 21, 12SS and Lehr Panzer Divisions in a piecemeal fashion to cover Caen, and to attack between the Orne and the Dives, instead of concentrating them for a strong offensive. In the Cherbourg Peninsula, he no doubt counted on the available German forces, which were to be reinforced by 3 Parachute and 77 Infantry Divisions from Brittany, to withstand any Allied offensive directed against Cherbourg.

By 12 June, the Allied bridgehead was soundly established, with a depth varying from eight to 12 miles, and the strength of the German counter-attacks on the west side of Caen suggested that the plan to attract Rommel's reserves to the Allied eastern flank was already proving effective.

Most importantly, no reserves had arrived in Normandy from north of the Seine. For those making the journey (2 Panzer Division), a long detour via Paris was involved because of the lack of bridges over the Seine. Moreover, through the efficiency of the Allied air reconnaissance, and the information from ULTRA sources, such movements were subjected to constant Allied air attack.

The weather remained a great anxiety. In continuing adverse conditions, it was greatly to the credit of the navies that the build-up was maintained. During the first six days there had been landed across the Normandy beaches 326,000 men, 54,000 vehicles and 104,000 tons of stores of all kinds.

Churchill in France
Montgomery steps ashore from the launch bringing Winston Churchill, Gen. Sir Alan Brooke, Gen. Jan Smuts and Rear-Adm. Barry to his head-quarters in France; 12 June 1944.

Montgomery's Headquarters

For the period immediately preceding D-Day, the Allied naval and air staffs moved to a location just outside Portsmouth. Eager to be as close as possible to events on the battlefield, Montgomery decided to move his Tactical HQ (Command Post) from England to Creully in Normandy. The Main HQ, consisting mainly of the Operations and Intelligence Staffs, along with an RAF liaison group, had to remain at Portsmouth until the essential radio, W/T and telephone communications facilities could be installed in Normandy. During this period the Chief of Staff was in charge in Portsmouth. On most days I flew over to Creully in a DC-3 Dakota in order to liaise with Montgomery: on other days my colleague Bill Williams would make the trip. Neither of us could leave the Portsmouth HQ until, above all else, the air forces' communications were fully established on the Continent.

Montgomery's transfer to northern France was not without its humorous side. He left Portsmouth on the evening of D-Day aboard HMS *Faulknor*, and the following day the senior commanders met aboard various warships making their way across the Channel. When the time came for Montgomery to disembark at his destination east of Arromanches, he was so anxious to be taken as close inshore as possible that *Faulknor* went aground and Montgomery completed his trip in an amphibious DUKW. Happily *Faulknor* was quickly refloated with some help from a tug – but I do not think that the Commander-in-Chief was the most popular senior officer carried to France by the Royal Navy.

Montgomery's HQ remained at Creully until 22 June, when he moved to Blay, six miles west of Bayeux in the American Sector, in order to be nearer General Bradley's First US Army HQ at Grandcamp-les-Bains, situated on the coast not far from OMAHA beach.

Maquis commander
Montgomery pauses on his way through a Normandy village to question one of the local maquis commanders whose unit had recently taken a number of German prisoners.

THE DEVELOPMENT OF THE BRIDGEHEAD: 13–19 JUNE

The Western (US) Sector *

During the early part of June, the American troops fighting in the western sector received welcome reinforcement with the arrival in Normandy of 19 US Corps and 8 US Corps. HQ 19 US Corps took the field on 14 June on the right of the OMAHA area with 2 Armoured, 29 and 30 US Divisions under command: HQ 8 US Corps became operational on 15 June, and took 90 Infantry and the airborne 82 and 101 Divisions under command, with responsibility for the southern part of what had been the UTAH area.

Rommel still placed great importance on breaking the junction between the US forces in the peninsula and those east of the River Vire, and for this purpose, immediately on its arrival from Poitiers, he directed 17SS Panzer Grenadier Division (motorized infantry) to the Carentan sector. The division did not however arrive at the front until late on 11 June. Allied air attacks had delayed the arrival of its assault guns, and the division was suffering from an acute shortage of vehicle fuel. It was not ready to launch an attack towards Carentan until 13 June, when it was thrown back by 101 US Airborne Division, assisted by tanks from 2 US Armoured.

Meanwhile, 4 US Division was fighting with commendable vigour around Montebourg. The town of Quinéville, on the coast, was captured and the enemy troops in Montebourg were forced to draw back to avoid being outflanked.

The enemy's concentration on the defence of Montebourg, and on efforts to break through to Carentan, had left a weakness in the area to the northwest of Ste-Mère-Eglise and the Americans were not slow to take advantage of this. On 14 June, 9 US Division, with units from 82 Airborne Division, forced its way westwards; on 16 June, troops of 82 Airborne occupied St-Sauveur and then wheeled south to protect the left flank while 9 Division burst through to the coast, which was reached on 18 June at Barneville-sur-Mer. Cherbourg was now cut off from the south: its further defence depended entirely on four weakened German divisions.

The newly arrived HQ 19 US Corps directed 29 and 30 US Divisions in the offensive towards St-Lô, but the enemy defences were strong: all bridges over the Taute–Vire canal had been blown and the defensive positions were protected by minefields. But 29 US Division on the right (east) bank of the Vire made excellent progress. By 18 June, the US forces in the Cherbourg Peninsula had three divisions (4, 9 and 82 Airborne) facing north from Barneville under 7 US Corps, while facing south there were 8, 19 and 5 US Corps, with a line running through the flooded, marshy country on the north side of la Haye-du-Puits and St-Lô, to Caumont, where 1 US Division was now established.

Sniper lure
An American soldier on foot patrol raises his helmet in an attempt to draw fire from a sniper. Further along the lane his colleagues advance cautiously, hoping to out-flank the hidden enemy.

The Eastern (British) Sector

It will be recalled that Second British Army's aim was to endeavour to encircle the city of Caen by a major thrust of 30 Corps through Villers-Bocage. With the deployment of 51 Highland Division in the bridgehead east of the River Orne, together with 6 Airborne, an offensive southwards was planned with the intention of developing a pincer movement in conjunction with the 30 Corps operation. But the determination of the Germans to hold on to Caen was evident; on 13 June both 21 Panzer and 12SS Panzer Division were on station covering the north side of the city.

7 British Armoured Division had been ordered to seize the high ground northeast of Villers-Bocage, while 50 Division was to follow through to take the town. Villers-Bocage was reached, but 2 Panzer Division, newly arrived from Amiens after a long detour via Paris, counter-attacked, and after confused fighting 7 Armoured Division had to pull back. At the end of 13 June, the British were still held north of Tilly and Villers-Bocage.

German 2 Panzer Division launched renewed counter-attacks during the afternoon of 14 June and pressed home the offensive until nearly midnight – forcing 7 British Armoured Division to give ground once again despite a very bitter and prolonged fight in which, at one point, 5 US Corps artillery switched their direction of fire across the army boundary to assist the hard-pressed 7 Armoured.

The battle raged back and forth for a period of four days and nights, but eventually, after a particularly violent engagement, the village of Tilly was taken on 19 June.

The pincer movement from *east* of the Orne made little progress. 51 Division captured Ste Honorine la Chardronnerette, but was evicted almost immediately by counter-attacks mounted by 346 German Division, with the aid of a battle group from 21 Panzer Division.

Due to the bad weather, the build-up schedule at the Allied beach-head was dropping further behind and the badly needed HQ 8 British Corps and the 11 Armoured Division were two days late when they began unloading on 15 June.

The Situation on 18 June

By 18 June, the Germans had four Panzer divisions in action in the British Sector between Caen and Caumont, these being 2, 12SS, 21 and Lehr. The 17SS Panzer Grenadier Division of mobile infantry was positioned south of Carentan, in the US Sector. Three fresh infantry divisions were also identified on the Allied front; 3 Parachute, deployed southeast of St-Lô, and 77 with 353 in the Peninsula.

For the Allies, the great worry was the continuing bad weather, which was causing increasing delays to the build-up at a time when additional strength would have made possible faster progress before the Germans found the means to reinforce their defences. The only consolation was that the policy adopted for delaying the enemy build-up was succeeding to a remarkable degree. The destruction of enemy command posts with their radio, wireless and telephone communications, and the relentless attacks on their road movements, railway entraining centres and military installations, gave the Allies a tremendous advantage, which was increased by the ever increasing sabotage activities of the French Resistance groups – aided by SAS troops and equipment flown in from Britain.

Montgomery's aim, always in accord with the framework of the master plan, was for First US Army to commence a movement due south towards the area Granville–Avranches–Vire, without awaiting the fall of Cherbourg. It was hoped that by 24 June HQ 15 US Corps would be operational, and that as soon as three more divisions had come ashore, 15 Corps could handle this offensive. Second British Army was to maintain its objective – to capture Caen by means of a pincer movement. From the west, the attack would be launched from a bridgehead to be seized over the River Odon, after which the troops would advance due east. The other arm of the pincer attack was to be launched from the bridgehead east of the Orne and to proceed round the east side of the city.

But experience showed that it would not be possible to deploy a whole corps in the space of the Orne bridgehead, which was very exposed and subject to continual enemy shelling. The plan was therefore altered. The movement from the west became the responsibility of HQ 8 British Corps, which was now operational, employing 15, 43 and 11 Armoured Divisions. 1 British Corps was to launch a direct thrust on Caen from the north and northwest, with 3 British and 3 Canadian Divisions respectively. At the same time and despite the superiority of the German opposition, 51 Division, positioned east of the Orne, was to take any opportunity it could to push southwards, leaving Caen on its right flank.

The intention was to launch these operations on 18 June. But certain types of artillery ammunition were in short supply, owing to unloading delays on the beaches, and the date had to be put back to 22 June. In the event, all plans were upset by a storm of unprecedented violence which lasted from 19 to 22 June.

Direct hit
An ammunition lorry explodes in a ball of flame after taking a direct hit from enemy mortar fire during an Allied attack towards the Odon River.

Development of the bridgehead

-------- Front on 9 June

———— Front on 18 June

Panzer division

Events on 18 June sealed the fate of Cherbourg, for on that day elements of 9 Division captured Barneville-sur-Mer on the west coast of the peninsula, isolating the port and preventing any chance of reinforcement.

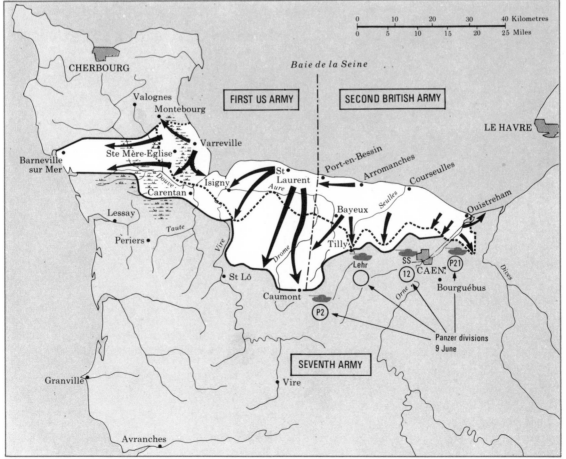

0　　　10　　　20　　　30　　　40 Kilometres
0　　5　　10　　15　　20　　25 Miles

Baie de la Seine

CHERBOURG

LE HAVRE

FIRST US ARMY

SECOND BRITISH ARMY

Valognes

Montebourg

Varreville

Ste Mère-Eglise

Barneville
sur Mer

Isigny

Carentan

Douve

St
Laurent

Aure

Port-en-Bessin

Arromanches

Courseulles

Seulles

Bayeux

Ouistreham

Lessay

Taute

Vire

Drome

Tilly

Lehr

SS
12

CAEN

P21

Dives

Periers

St Lô

Caumont

Orne

Bourguébus

P2

Panzer divisions
9 June

Granville

Vire

SEVENTH ARMY

Avranches

The Psychology of Command

It is interesting to note here the weakness that may be created in an otherwise effective fighting unit, simply through the habitual behaviour patterns of the men involved.

Through studying the siting of German Divisional, Corps and other headquarters in Normandy, we learned that a German general invariably set up his Command Post in a château or other comfortable and imposing residence in the rear of his sector of the front. When our intelligence staff discovered – from prisoner-of-war interrogation – the divisional or other boundaries of a formation, we immediately searched on air photographs for a likely looking rearward Command Post. Often these would be disclosed by nearby wireless trucks or staff transport vehicles: occasionally a low-level photo-reconnaissance run would be requested. But as soon as an enemy HQ location was identified, the tactical air forces would be informed – and the building would be destroyed. This 'human failing' contributed in no small way to the high level of German losses at senior command level: during the battle for Normandy the German Army lost no fewer than 20 generals, killed or taken prisoner, in addition to two who were known to have been seriously wounded in raids on command centres.

By contrast, Montgomery's small Command Post was always sited in the forward area so that he was readily available for consultations with his senior subordinate commanders, and in close radio range with them. He used a converted lorry as an office and sleeping quarters, together with a 'map-room' trailer. The staff and signal-communications personnel usually bedded down in small bivouac tent shelters. The location was always in the open country, often

Under pressure
*Field-Marshals Rommel
and Von Rundstedt meet
to discuss the situation in
northwestern France.*

near a small village. The main HQ, comprising the Operations and
Planning Staff, and senior personnel of the administration departments, was also sited in an open field location, well protected by
camouflage nets. (Our first 'address' in Normandy was in an apple
orchard, near Bayeux.)

The Operations Staff included an element responsible for close
co-operation with the tactical air force HQ and, as in North Africa,
and again in Sicily and Italy, we worked with Air Vice Marshal
Broadhurst's 83 Group RAF. We had a formal meeting every evening
to review the day's operations and to discuss plans for the following
day, and it may be of interest to elaborate here on the system of
co-operation between us.

Sometime on D+3 or D+4 I discovered from air reconnaissance
reports that nearly all German troop movements were on secondary
routes, and it occurred to me to get hold of a French 'Michelin' map.
On these maps main roads are marked in red, and second-class roads
in yellow. In virtually all cases, our air reports indicated that the
Germans were using the 'yellow' routes. We were thus able to pin-
point the main bottlenecks on the yellow roads leading to the
German delivery points, where ammunition, vehicle fuel, stores and
rations were probably off-loaded by night. At a meeting with Sir
Arthur Tedder it was arranged that bombing raids would be made at
these bottlenecks – as late in the day as possible – using cratering
bombs and high-explosive missiles to pile up rubble. At first light the
fighter-bombers made sorties to the bottlenecks. The plan proved
successful. Invariably the destruction of the night raids had caused
heavy traffic congestion at the target areas, leaving the enemy
supply convoys stranded and unable to avoid the dawn strikes by the
tactical air force.

THE CAPTURE OF CHERBOURG AND THE ESTABLISHMENT OF THE ODON BRIDGEHEAD: 19–30 JUNE

Allied objectives at 19 June

Montgomery's orders on 18 June instructed First US Army to complete the capture of Cherbourg and to clear the peninsula, in order that it could then concentrate all its forces (which now comprised 5, 7, 8 and 19 US Corps) facing south. Once the whole of General Bradley's army was relieved of its preoccupation with the capture of Cherbourg, the entire Anglo-American bridgehead would be arraigned in line. Then, providing Second British Army could continue to attract the main German reserves – particularly the Panzer Divisions – to the Allies' east flank, First American Army would be poised to break out southwards to seal off Brittany and so achieve the next phase of the master plan.

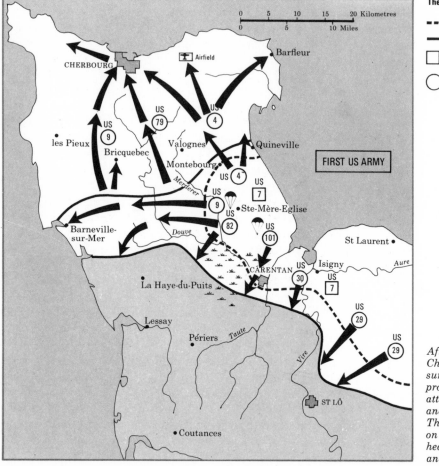

The capture of Cherbourg

- - - - - Front line 3 June
——— Front line 18 June
☐ Corps
◯ Division

After stubborn resistance, Cherbourg finally surrendered to a three-pronged American ground attack supported by air and naval bombardment. The town was surrendered on 26 June (right) with heavy losses in men killed and taken prisoner.

The Fall of Cherbourg

The attempts of the Americans to strike southwards while still occupied with the capture of Cherbourg had not proved practical. The Germans had reinforced their units facing the Carentan area and, in particular, 17SS Panzer Grenadier Division had at last deployed in the sector, in spite of the heavy casualties suffered in Allied air attacks throughout its journey from south of the Loire. Consequently it was decided not to make any further attempt to strike south, but to hold the front until the peninsula was cleared.

In the north, 4 US Division made a surprise attack on 19 June, and seized the high ground northwest of Montebourg. The town itself was not captured until the evening, but by nightfall the division had pressed home its advantage and was on the outskirts of Valognes. In the centre of the peninsula, 79 US Division struck north between Valognes and Bricquebec, while 9 US Division made excellent progress on the west flank to reach a point only eight miles southwest of Cherbourg.

The three US divisions progressively closed in on the city, and launched a co-ordinated assault on 22 June. The attack opened with a heavy air bombardment of the defensive positions, but although damage and casualties were high, the defending troops showed stubborn resistance – following Hitler's orders that the port be defended to the last man. The airfield at Maupertus, a few miles east of Cherbourg, was taken on 23 June, and by the following day American units were closing on the outskirts of the city. Only after a prolonged and bitter engagement, in which the city was subjected to a barrage of fire from the air, from naval support ships, and from ground artillery, did the German garrison commander and the naval commander surrender on 26 June. And even then, small pockets of resistance held out for two more days – not knowing of the surrender order due to the destruction of their communication system. The final clearance of the outlying areas in the northwest corner of the peninsula was completed on 1 July and 7 US Corps was finally free to withdraw to the south to join the troops holding the southern front on the line from Barneville through Carentan to Caumont.

Behind them they left the port of Cherbourg in the hands of the clearance teams – faced with the enormous task of reopening the port. Such was the extent of the wrecking and mining of port installations and anchorages that it was late August before the first Allied supply ships were able to berth at Cherbourg.

The Odon Bridgehead: Codename EPSOM

The efforts to seize Caen, or to surround the city as a prelude to its seizure, continued. Although still in enemy hands, the city was fulfilling the role hoped for in the master plan. 12SS and 21 Panzer Divisions, with 716 Infantry Division, were covering the approaches to Caen from our bridgehead east of the Orne, and from the north and northwest, while Panzer Lehr and 2 Panzer Divisions were deployed to resist any British thrust from the area of Tilly–Caumont designed to swing round the south of Caen.

It had been intended to launch the next major British attack on 22 June, preceded by another attack by 51 Division from the bridgehead east of the River Orne as a diversionary operation. The main offensive was to be undertaken by 30 Corps on the British right flank. 49 Infantry Division, with tank support, was to attack from east of Tilly, with the high ground around Rauray as its first objective. Eventually General Dempsey hoped to exploit to Noyers-Bocage, and thence advance to the River Odon at Aunay. Meanwhile, 8 Corps was to attack from the area of le Mesnil-Patry on a southward centre-line through Cheux–Colleville–Tourville-sur-Odon, and then across the Odon to Baron-sur-Odon and the high ground to its east. 8 Corps had 7 and 11 Armoured and 15 and 43 Infantry Divisions for its task, while two further armoured brigades (six regiments) were

The Odon bridgehead

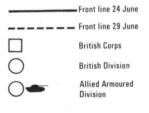

—————— Front line 24 June

— — — — — — Front line 29 June

☐   British Corps

◯   British Division

◯   Allied Armoured Division

held in reserve. Montgomery's intention was to exploit the advance to the River Orne and thus cut off all routes into Caen from the south.

Most unfortunately, the whole concept had to be delayed owing to the appalling weather. The gale which raged from June 19 to June 22 had the effect of imposing a week's delay in our build-up programme over the beaches, but eventually, on 23 June, 51 Division carried out its attack and recaptured Ste Honorine. This provoked a full-scale counter-attack by 21 Panzer Division, which was repulsed. The attention of 12SS Panzer Division was meanwhile distracted by local attacks north and northwest of Caen by 3 British and 3 Canadian Divisions.

30 Corps began its thrust on 25 June, and 8 Corps on 26 June. There followed a period of intense fighting, which continued until 30 June, by which time 30 Corps had reached Rauray and Tessel, but could not maintain its momentum in the difficult *bocage* country against 2SS Panzer Division.

8 Corps secured a bridge intact over the Odon near Baron, and by 30 June was holding a bridgehead over the river about two and a half miles long but no more than one mile in depth. On 29 June, both 1SS and 2SS Panzer Divisions were encountered on this front, together with advance elements of 10SS Panzer Division transferred from the Russian front. There were thus, by the end of June, no less than eight Panzer divisions on the twenty-mile frontage of the Second British Army between Caumont and Caen.

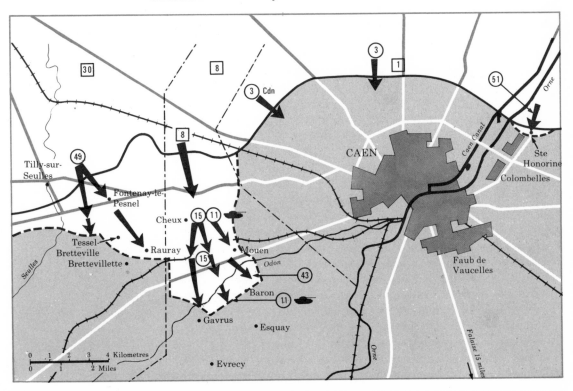

Against such opposition, Second Army was obliged to concentrate on holding the ground won, and to await the reinforcements that had been so grievously delayed by the storm of 19–22 June. In a short spell of reorganization, the infantry took over the front so that 7 and 11 Armoured Divisions could be concentrated in reserve, ready for renewed offensives.

THE GREAT SET-BACK

The delay in starting Second Army's offensive, originally planned for 22 June, had far-reaching effects on the conduct of operations. On 18 June, the weather began deteriorating, and by the following day the northeasterly gale had reached 30 knots, and at sea the waves were six to eight feet high. The storm persisted until 22 June, and was the worst on record in the English Channel for 40 years.

All ship-to-shore operations were brought to a complete halt. More than 800 craft were stranded, and many destroyed or badly damaged. On the Normandy beaches the situation was chaotic – saved from being a total disaster only by the Gooseberry breakwaters. At Arromanches, where considerable progress had been made with the construction of the Mulberry harbour, the main breakwater held and some 500 landing craft and other vessels found shelter from the elements. Without this relief, the loss of small landing craft might well have crippled the future operation in the Arromanches sector. Construction of the other Mulberry off St-Laurent was not as advanced, and by 21 June the main breakwater had lost most of its protective value. Owing to tidal scour, many of the blockships settled on the sands, and of 30 caissons, only ten remained fit for utilization: the two piers which were taking shape when the storm began were completely written off, mainly by the impact of landing craft thrown against them by the seas.

The following statistics give some idea of the effect of the storm on the build-up programme. Between 15 and 18 June, at OMAHA and UTAH, 19,000 men and 3,000 vehicles were landed; between 19 and 22 June, the corresponding figures were 6,000 men and 1,000 vehicles. Similar effects were experienced on GOLD, JUNO and SWORD where the cumulative delay resulted in the British build-up being *three divisions* behind schedule by as much as one week.

The enemy had virtually four days' grace in which to bring forward reinforcement divisions, because the air forces were inhibited in providing the normal degree of support and attacks on enemy movements were restricted. During the period of the storm, 2 Panzer Division took station in the Caumont area, 352 Division got into action south of Carentan and 3 Para Division completed its concentration opposite the west flank of First US Army.

Though the storm abated on 23 June, the Allied air forces were still hampered by thick cloud and dense mist, which greatly reduced

Storm damage
The storm of 18–22 June did enormous damage and the Allies were fortunate that a muddled German High Command did not take advantage of the situation. Fuel and supply barges (right) were hurled together and the artificial harbour off St. Laurent (below) was so badly damaged that it was never brought into operation.

visibility at ground level. Only 83 Group RAF could assist Second Army's offensive when it got started on 25 and 26 June. The Group made 500 sorties on 26 June in spite of the appalling flying conditions, while 9 US Air Force also made sorties in support of First US Army. But the move to Normandy of 1SS Panzer Division from Belgium was not impeded to the expected degree. On 28 June, the Luftwaffe made some showing in the British sector, but 83 Group shot down 26 German aircraft on that day.

On the same day the first prisoners were captured – from 2SS Panzer Division, which had been brought up from Toulouse. The Germans had intended to deploy 2SS in the Carentan sector, opposite First US Army, but instead it was switched to reinforce the resistance to the 8 British Corps offensive. In the steady build-up of defensive formations, 9SS and 10SS Panzer Divisions, newly arrived from the Russian front after a long and exhausting journey, were also committed against 8 Corps.

By 29 June, the attempted encirclement movement to the south of Caen by Second British Army was fast losing momentum and every available means of fire support was concentrated to assist the manoeuvre. The RAF flew 1,000 sorties; the naval gun-fire was described as 'murderous', and artillery was switched from both 1 and 30 Corps, while Bomber Command dropped 1,000 tons of bombs on the enemy at night. Nevertheless, 8 Corps had to stop the offensive on 30 June. The mass of German armour drawn up in this sector was quite impenetrable. From radio interceptions, Allied intelligence had been able to assess the German tank strength facing the Allies. Against the British sector there were 725 tanks: against the American sector there were 140. The enemy was reacting as intended. The available fire-power of German Seventh Army was being drawn into the Caen area and the scene was being set for the US break-out to the south, in order to cut off Brittany.

During this period the Allied navies were principally concerned with the U-boat offensive. Hitler had ordered that all Allied naval resources should be obliterated, but up to 30 June only four U-boats had penetrated as far as 'The Spout'. HMS *Goodson* was sunk, together with four landing ships, but of 25 U-boats ordered into the Channel, 12 were sunk, eight returned to base, and the remaining five proceeded up to the North Sea. German torpedo boats had, by 30 June, ceased to be a problem to the Allied sea crossing from England. By the end of June, when the fleet warships had to thin out (many being required in the south of France to support the Allied invasion due to take place there in early August), the transfer of personnel and stores to France from the UK since D-Day had reached 850,000 men, 149,000 vehicles and 570,000 tons of stores, in spite of the bad weather and the damage to the Mulberry harbours. Indeed the Mulberry at St-Laurent had to be abandoned, but the Arromanches artificial harbour was repaired and continued to give valuable service during the development of the bridgehead.

Arromanches
All the principal elements in the Gooseberry and Mulberry design concepts can be picked out in this air photograph of the Arromanches harbour.

The Situation on 30 June

Montgomery took stock of the Allied position and was well pleased with the progress achieved. The Germans had tried to liquidate the incursion of the Allied forces by using 21, 12SS and Lehr Panzer Divisions between the Orne and Vire, meanwhile isolating the Cherbourg Peninsula in order to annihilate US 5 Corps by reinforcing the troops in the peninsula. This concept had failed.

Von Rundstedt and Rommel had decided to concentrate a powerful armoured force to seal off the Allied bridgehead, but due to highly effective air force participation and naval gunfire support, it took over a fortnight to gather the German formations for a concentrated drive to crush the Allied offensives. The enemy high command had brought into action 1SS, 2SS, 2, 9SS and 10SS Panzer divisions. Had they been concentrated under a single command they could have launched a formidable offensive, but the concentration was never realized. The 8 British Corps thrust, supported by secondary offensive actions by 30 Corps on the east flank – north of Caumont – and by 1 Corps northeast of Caen and 51 Division east of the Orne, had forced the Germans to commit the arriving Panzer formations piecemeal, in order to hold the Allied initiatives.

There were now grouped eight German Panzer divisions (less a battle group south of St-Lô) for the defence of Caen, but Von Rundstedt's crust-cushion-hammer tactics had failed at all stages. On the other hand, Montgomery had to devise, quickly, some means of retaining the enemy armoured troops on the Allied east flank. Now that First US Army had completed the task of capturing Cherbourg and was able to concentrate on the southern front, it required only to secure the general line St-Lô–Périers–Lessay (on the west coast of the peninsula) and it would be ready for the next stage of the master plan.

The Germans, however, had problems, despite the strength of the eight élite armoured divisions in Normandy. The *bocage* country was not suitable for mobile operations, and they had been unable to bring in sufficient infantry to make any serious offensive move in the eastern sector. The Panzer divisions were short of petrol and ammunition due to Allied air attacks on their replenishment columns, and they had lost a proportion of their artillery for the same reason. The petrol problem applied to all enemy forces; through air attacks, mainly by 8 US Air Force, vehicle fuel production in Germany had dropped by 40 per cent and very little of what was being produced was reaching the Normandy battle zone.

There had still been no known transfer of infantry divisions from north of the Seine, and it had to be assumed that Hitler still believed that a second Allied front would be opened in the Pas de Calais. Yet without more infantry in Normandy, Von Rundstedt could not relieve his Panzer divisions for more mobile operations on the western flank. Moreover, as long as his armour was pinned down on the defensive, the greater their losses would be through the Allied air and naval bombardments, and because of lack of spares and workshop attention.

The availability of reinforcements for the German Army was also limited because, from whatever region they came, they *had* to pass through the Chartres gap (between the Seine and Loire), which was vulnerable to air attack and to increasingly effective French sabotage action. One example of the delays thus caused was the move of 9SS and 10SS Panzer Divisions from the Russian front to Normandy: it took them longer to reach the Caen sector from the French frontier than it had to cover the journey from Poland to France. In considering this factor, it is of interest to speculate about the success which might have been achieved at Caen, had it not been for the appalling weather conditions in the second half of June. There seems little doubt that the encirclement of Caen would have been achieved by the Allies long before enemy reinforcements reached the combat zone. On the other hand, the delay enabled the British forces to 'absorb' the Panzer divisions piecemeal in the fighting for Caen, whereas without it more armour might have been diverted to the US front, which is exactly what Montgomery sought to avoid.

It may be added that at one point (it was at a meeting of the Allied Air Commanders on 14 June) Sir Arthur Tedder began to have misgivings about the Allied Army's progress and expressed the fear that the situation 'had the makings of a dangerous crisis', because Caen had not been captured; the army had not squared up to the River Dives on the east, and no progress had been made towards securing airfield country south of Caen.

Those who thought that Montgomery's master plan had failed, or was failing, completely misunderstood the situation. Certainly it had

The situation on 30 June

Front line 30 June

US — US Corps

Brit — British Corps

Allied Armoured Division

Ger — German Corps

German Division

German Airborne Division

German Armoured Division

German Grenadiers

been hoped to capture Caen on D-Day; but this was not because the town itself had any great military or intrinsic value to the Allies. Taking the town was intended to confirm German suspicions that the Allied breakout was to be made from the Caen region, and thereby to oblige the commitment of the German armour to that area. This would, in Montgomery's view, prevent the concentration of the enemy for a thrust to the coast, and would relieve the Americans of armoured intervention in order to accelerate their break-out to the south. The whole concept was based on total defeat of the Germans in Normandy. Although Caen had not been captured it had, to date, fulfilled its purpose, since eight Panzer divisions were deployed to defend it. The master plan was not jeopardized: on the contrary, it was proceeding well. Whatever gave Sir Arthur Tedder his misgivings on 14 June is difficult to understand. If they were due to delays in capturing the airfield country south of Caen, he had a point – but surely not a major one, since the Allied air forces were playing a very significant part in the battle, both strategically and tactically, and in terms of interdiction, the protection of shipping and direct support of the land battle.

Montgomery's real problem at 30 June was to retain the initiative which had forced the Germans to 'plug holes' instead of concentrating their forces for an effective *schwerpunkt*, and thereby to keep the German armoured divisions on the Allies' eastern flank.

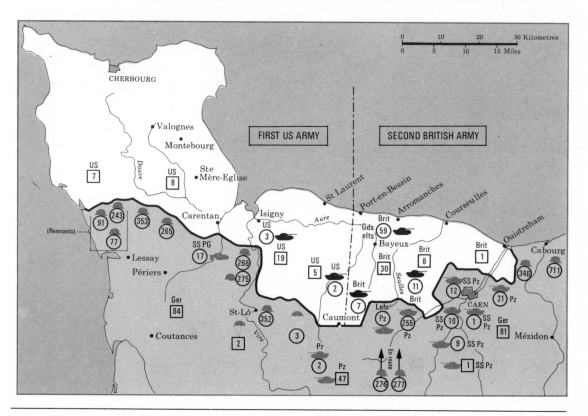

PART VI

The Break-out

PREPARATIONS FOR OPERATION 'COBRA'

On 30 June, Montgomery issued his battle orders for the development of the Normandy campaign. Allied operations were rapidly building up to a climax: a point at which it would very soon be known whether or not the plan for a complete encirclement of German Seventh Army would prove viable.

First US Army was required to take advantage of the existing enemy dispositions to stage the break-out (codenamed COBRA) southwards from the bridgehead. Montgomery rather optimistically set the date for 3 July. Second British Army was to continue its operation aimed at the capture of Caen and to maintain maximum offensive pressure throughout the eastern sector to prevent the transfer of any Panzer divisions to the US First Army Front. It had, in addition, to guard against any concerted enemy counter-attack as any such attack, if successful, could throw the entire Allied front out of balance. If Rommel were to receive sufficient infantry reinforcements to free his armoured divisions for a massive thrust to the coast, the Allies would be in great difficulties.

Command meeting
General Montgomery and General Bradley, Senior Commander, U.S. Ground Forces, hold a roadside conference in Normandy.

First US Army

Speed was the essential factor, for as long as there was only one regimental group of Panzer troops on the US front, and eight Panzer divisions committed in the British sector, the more propitious were the conditions for First Army to burst through to the south, on a front pivoting on Caumont. Montgomery and Bradley agreed that the first phase should be to swing on to a line running through Vire–Mortain–Fougères.

Montgomery's idea was that if First Army could reach that line, progress could be made to a new front, Mayenne–Laval, and thence Alençon–Le Mans, while a subsidiary operation would be launched to Vannes to cut off Brittany. From that point, his forward thinking was that the Chartres gap, between the Loire and the Seine, should be closed to the enemy by dropping an Allied airborne division there. The entire German Seventh Army in Normandy would then be trapped with no bridges over the Seine west of Paris by which they could make their escape.

In the event, there was no way of avoiding the frustrating delays imposed upon General Bradley. Before First US Army could launch a major and continuous offensive, Bradley had to secure a suitable starting line upon which to deploy his assaulting divisions, and which would also ensure communications for the follow-through formations. The extent of the flooded marshy country associated with the Carentan estuary made it necessary to advance to a line Périers–St-Lô. As may be imagined, the enemy resistance in such ideally defensive country made progress extremely slow. To the difficulties of the *bocage* country were added the persistently unfavourable weather conditions which restricted air support. The US troops in these operations suffered heavy casualties.

While 7 US Corps was completing the capture of Cherbourg at the end of June, preparations for the break-out began. On 3 July, 8 US Corps attacked la Haye-du-Puits, but it was 8 July before 79 US Division finally secured the town. Meanwhile, 7 US Corps, having returned to the southern front, attacked southwest of Carentan and made some progress, but 83 Division was counter-attacked in the area by 2SS Panzer Division, which had been hurriedly switched from the Odon.

Montgomery was becoming increasingly anxious about the western flank, and had to devise further initiatives to prevent the transfer of Panzer divisions to oppose the Americans. There were also increasingly firm indications that Rommel was preparing to launch a major counter-stroke aimed at driving a wedge through the Allied bridgehead to the coast. His intended target remains unknown, although the most likely point at which to aim a *schwerpunkt* would have been at the boundary between First US and Second British Armies – thus destroying the cohesion of the Allied operation and endangering the entire bridgehead.

The Capture of Caen

On 1 July, the SS Panzer divisions made a concerted attack against the Second Army salient over the Odon River. 1, 2, 9, 10 and 12 SS Panzer Divisions, mainly very under strength, formed up with their tanks and Grenadier infantry and attacked astride Rauray, but after several days of fierce fighting, the enemy went over to the defensive having suffered severe casualties. This was by far the strongest of the many attacks which were launched and the fact that it was successfully repulsed owes much to the devastating volume of artillery fire directed from the Allied formations holding the Odon salient. 9SS Panzer Division alone lost 32 tanks in a bitter engagement with 49 Division supported by 8 Armoured Brigade.

On 3 and 4 July, it was learnt from prisoners captured in this engagement that the Germans were bringing infantry into our eastern flank, presumably to relieve armoured divisions. 16 GAF (German Air Force) Division was located east of the Orne, and 276 Division was brought into action in the Tilly-sur-Seulles sector.

Second Army made little progress to the east of Caen, but Carpiquet airfield was at last captured on 9 July.

Montgomery and Dempsey now came up with a new concept in order to capture Caen, and finally obtained the consent of Eisenhower to attempt an assault in conjunction with RAF Bomber Command. Such an attack had not previously been tried, and there were many problems to be resolved. Sir Arthur Harris, commanding Bomber Command, readily agreed to a joint study for such an enterprise, but the problem of establishing a safe night bomb-line for aircraft supporting ground troops had to be resolved, and the limit areas for cratering by delayed-fuse bombs, which were more effective against enemy defensive positions, had to be defined.

It was jointly decided that the bomb-line would be no nearer to the ground troops than 6,000 yards, which was thought to be a safe margin. The target area was a rectangle on the northern outskirts of Caen, 4,000 yards wide and 500 yards deep in the area known to contain enemy defensive and HQ locations. Between 2150 and 2230 hours on 7 July, 460 aircraft, each carrying a bomb load of five tons, made a remarkably accurate attack, eliminating most of the enemy gun emplacements and causing extensive damage to the HQ installations. At 0420 hours, the infantry attack by 3 and 59 British and 3 Canadian divisions began and after two days of heavy fighting the town of Caen west of the Orne was in our hands, although the suburb of Vaucelles, east of the river, was not captured – partly because all bridges over the River Orne had been blown.

Investigations showed that some German defenders were found still stunned many hours after the attack. Surviving German troops north of the town were left without food, petrol and ammunition, and one regiment of 16 GAF Division was completely wiped out. But the importance of the operation was that the capture of Caen had simplified the operational problems on the Allied flank, and having finally eliminated this determined enemy salient west of the Orne, operations could be planned for the extension of our restricted bridgehead east of the river, which was still held by the hard-pressed 6 Airborne and 51 Highland Divisions together with the Special Air Service units.

German policy was clearly designed to prevent the Allies from exploiting their power of mobility and manoeuvre in the open country south and southeast of Caen; from threatening the lateral west-east routes through Falaise and Argentan, vital for their supply and replenishment system; and from attempting a thrust towards Rouen or towards Paris. The key to retaining the Panzer forces in the east was therefore the establishment of a strong force southeast of Caen.

Montgomery decided that an attack east of the Orne from the restricted Allied bridgehead there, and secondly a renewed thrust from the River Odon to the River Orne south of Caen, should be undertaken as soon as possible. At the same time, he ordered Second British Army to take over the sector held by 5 US Corps, in order to provide General Bradley with additional resources for operation COBRA.

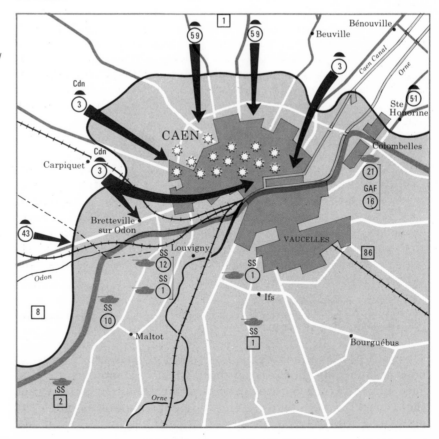

The Allied Front: 10–18 July

During this period, General Bradley's First US Army launched a series of attacks designed to clear the required 'jumping-off' area. 8 US Corps captured Lessay, after heavy fighting, on 14 July, while 7 US Corps advanced astride the River Taute. 19 US Corps fought its way forward between the Rivers Taute and Vire, and this Corps finally captured St-Lô on the evening of 17 July, in spite of a desperate counter-offensive by Panzer Lehr Division.

Thus, by 18 July, First US Army was established on a potential start-line for the break-out operation. But Bradley had informed Montgomery, at a meeting held on 10 July, that it would not be possible for a major operation to be launched before 20 July owing to the delayed arrival of artillery ammunition and other essential stores, which had to be stocked up to ensure adequate logistical backing for the intended offensive.

Second British Army had to keep up the pressure, and launched a series of strong attacks from its positions on the River Odon, and in the area of Tilly-sur-Seulles. The operations were conducted by six divisions, on as broad a front as possible, with the object of dispersing the German defensive resources and striking towards the River Orne south of Caen.

43 Division, together with an armoured brigade, captured Eterville on 10 July, but was unable to hold Maltot against strong counter-attacks by 9SS and 10SS Panzer Divisions. 49 and 50 Divisions made progress astride the River Seulles during 11 July, and on the same day 51 Division struck towards Colombelles east of the Orne, in an attack designed to commit 21 Panzer Division, which had been due to withdraw for a refit.

On 15 July, 12 Corps launched a night attack on Evrecy, using a new technique called 'Movement Light', which proved very successful. It relied, for ground illumination, on the reflection of searchlights from the very cloudy sky. Although Esquay–Notre-Dame was captured and retained, the German defenders of Evrecy stood firm.

As a result of these British attacks, 1SS, 9SS, 10SS and 21 Panzer Divisions were held in the east, although they were intended to be concentrated in the rear for refitting. In addition 2, 12SS, and 116 Panzer Divisions were also committed in the east, leaving only Lehr and 2SS Panzer Divisions in the west.

Delay in the Break-out

When, on 10 July, Bradley explained to Montgomery that he saw no hope of launching the break-out until 20 July, Montgomery had to accept the delay. He realized the difficulty of the terrain over which the Americans were fighting and fully appreciated the danger of launching COBRA before adequate logistical support was available.

On the other hand, he was anxious about the ability of the British and Canadian divisions to continue indefinitely to oblige the Germans to retain their Panzer divisions on the defensive in the eastern sector. More German infantry divisions were known to be on their way to the front; specifically 271 and 272 (both first-line formations) from the south of France. Moreover, it seemed impossible that Hitler could continue for much longer to envisage an assault in the Pas de Calais; and once he gave his assent to reinforcing Seventh German Army with troops from Fifteenth, very substantial reinforcements would be available for Normandy. In spite of the generally slow movement of German infantry formations they would eventually reach Normandy without, perhaps, the 'normal' punishment from the air forces during their displacement; the weather continued to favour the enemy.

Montgomery decided that the only way open to him for pinning down the enemy Panzer divisions on the eastern flank was the delivery of a tremendous thrust from our narrow bridgehead east of the River Orne, directed to by-pass Caen on the east side, and seemingly intended to create a saleint to the area of Falaise and beyond. Although we knew that Rommel had a defence system south of Caen disposed in no less than five defensive belts, he thought that a very heavy offensive supported by the strength of the Allied air forces would serve to confirm to the enemy that the intention of the Allies was a thrust towards the Seine and Paris. The time factor remained all important.

British operations west of the Orne: 10–18 July

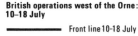

— Front line 10–18 July

☐ Corps   ◯ Division

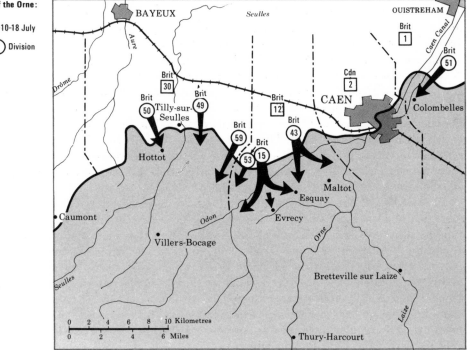

Operation GOODWOOD: 18–20 July

In the event, the earliest date by which such an offensive could be launched was 18 July, assuming that the Allied air forces would be ready and made available immediately. Montgomery asked Eisenhower for the maximum support of the strategical and tactical air forces. This support was granted, but the phrasing of Montgomery's request to Eisenhower created the impression at SHAEF that the British–Canadian initiative would be similar to that envisaged by Bradley on the western flank – that is, a full-scale break-out operation. Eisenhower in due course proclaimed that the Allies were poised to develop *two* concurrent break-out operations, and that from the eastern flank the exploitation would be made towards the Seine valley, and from the west southwards to the Biscay coast.

Nothing was further from Montgomery's mind than the idea of a break-out from the eastern wing. Even had it proved successful, it would have upset the whole concept of the master plan by destroying the encirclement plan. But when Eisenhower declared that the Allies were poised for a 'double' break-out, Montgomery did not comment, nor seek to correct the Supreme Commander, because he feared that the tremendous back-up of the strategic air forces would be denied him for a relatively 'local' operation which amounted to a battle for position.

The plan for what was called Operation GOODWOOD, was based on an offensive by three armoured divisions – Guards, 7, and 11 – advancing in line abreast, with the follow-up of four infantry divisions. The objective was the Bourgébus ridge some four and a half miles south of the centre of Caen. 11 Armoured was directed on Hubert-Folie; 7 Armoured on Bourgébus, and the Guards to the southeast towards Vimont. Bomber Command was briefed to neutralize German strong-points and battery locations on the flanks of the armoured attack corridor. The corridor itself was to be saturated by impact-fused shrapnel bombs by 9 US Air Force, and 8 US Air Force heavy bombers were to drop fragmentation bombs in the area south of the Bourgébus ridge. The 8th were also to obliterate Troarn on the River Dives. The tactical air force fighter-bombers would provide support to the ground forces by attacks on any enemy strongholds which proved to be hindering the Allied advance.

In retrospect, the Allies were seen to have underestimated the strength and extent of the enemy defences. The German front was held by infantry: behind them was the armour of 21 Panzer Division together with over 30 Tiger tanks (the most powerful tanks in Normandy) and a unit of 1SS Panzer Division. Farther back, lay a string of defended villages, and thereafter a gun-line of seventy-eight 88mm D.P. guns. The German artillery in the area comprised 200 field guns and nearly 300 mattress mortar-gun units. In retrospect we learnt that Rommel had yet another defence line, consisting of battle groups of 1SS and 12SS Panzer Divisions.

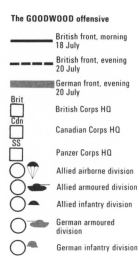

The GOODWOOD offensive

British front, morning 18 July

British front, evening 20 July

German front, evening 20 July

Brit — British Corps HQ

Cdn — Canadian Corps HQ

SS — Panzer Corps HQ

Allied airborne division

Allied armoured division

Allied infantry division

German armoured division

German infantry division

The battle was called off on the afternoon of 20 July, when a deluge of rain had swamped the terrain. But the operation had wholly achieved its object: it had succeeded in riveting the German forces to the eastern Allied front, and thus gained time for Bradley to make his break-out in favourable conditions. Foul weather again held up First US Army from 20 July to 24 July – and on that day, restricted visibility caused a short-fall on the bomb line during the preliminary air action – but the break-out at last began on 25 July.

The GOODWOOD operation was thus fully justified, in spite of the heavy casualties sustained by the Second British Army. On 15 July, the German forces facing the American west wing totalled 190 tanks and 85 infantry battalions: on the British–Canadian front, there were massed 645 tanks and 92 infantry battalions.

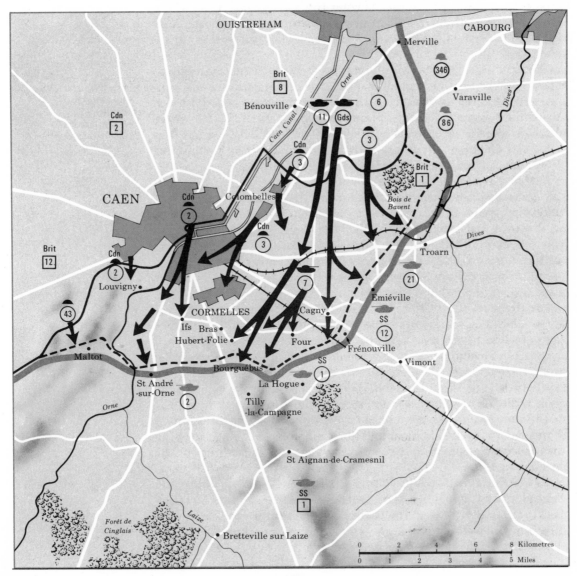

The Argument over GOODWOOD

The master plan was succeeding. But the senior commanders at Eisenhower's HQ were anything but satisfied. There now arose the first major disagreement between Eisenhower and Montgomery. The former and his staff, from Tedder (his deputy) downwards, thought that the GOODWOOD offensive had failed. The misunderstanding began when the case for the co-operation of all the Allied air forces was based on the assumption that Montgomery intended to break out to Falaise and beyond. In fact, Montgomery had given a personal memorandum to General O'Connor, the Commander of 8 Corps, in which he stipulated that the objective was to wear down the German armour and to extend the bridgehead east of the Orne. O'Connor was *not* to proceed beyond the Bourgébus ridge: if the enemy were to withdraw, O'Connor was authorized to send armoured car patrols forward to determine the enemy's situation – but no more.

The air forces felt that Montgomery's failure to break through to Falaise and beyond, in order to capture the airfield sites, was a 'sellout' after all the co-operation they had afforded Second British Army. Sir Arthur Tedder complained to Eisenhower that the latter should approach the British Chiefs of Staff with his misgivings about the command structure in Normandy, and that Eisenhower should himself assume direct command of operations.

On 20 July, Eisenhower met with Montgomery and Bradley, having meanwhile passed on to Churchill his fears about the command direction in Normandy. It was said that Eisenhower expressed his disappointment about GOODWOOD; but at the same meeting he also learnt that Bradley had been forced to delay his thrust yet again – until 25 July. It was clear that Eisenhower was no longer judging the operational situation in terms of the original master plan.

On the same day Churchill visited Montgomery, and at once agreed that the progress of the plan was highly satisfactory, and that a great victory was awaiting the Allies. After his visit Churchill reassured Eisenhower, but Tedder and Morgan remained unimpressed. It must be admitted that there was a clash of personalities between Air Chief Marshal Tedder and Montgomery, but none of us in the HQ Staff has ever determined the reason for it. I can only testify that I do not think it arose from any action or statement by Montgomery. He would have told his operations staff had that been the case; what he did say was that he deeply regretted the circumstance.

Earlier in this account I have spoken of the difficulties and misunderstandings which arose within the Allied command structure through a failure on the part of several senior commanders to fully appreciate the fundamental concept of Montgomery's conduct of the Normandy campaign. The bitter conflict over GOODWOOD

Situation report
Lt.-Gen. Simmonds, Prime Minister Churchill, Gen. Montgomery and Gen. Dempsey review the progress of the Allied offensive after the fall of Caen.

is a prime example. This offensive was launched purely and simply to prevent the transfer of Panzer divisions from the British Sector to Bradley's front in the west. When Bradley had to postpone his break-out date from 20 July until 25 July, Montgomery realized that the overall plan was endangered. He knew from intelligence reports that the German Army had brought three new infantry divisions (16 GAF, 276 and 277) into the line in order to allow 1SS, 2, Lehr and 21 Panzer Divisions to be transferred to the American front. At all costs, Montgomery had to prevent this, and with commendable speed he set up a force of three armoured and four infantry divisions, supported by a tremendous air offensive programme – *not* to break out of the bridgehead, as apparently Eisenhower and Tedder thought, but to hold the German armour by a very limited but concentrated attack to the Bourgébus ridge. He succeeded in his purpose: all the German armoured divisions were immediately thrown back into the line and there remained only some 190 tanks on Bradley's front.

First US Army lines up

During the first week of July, in spite of the efforts of Second British and First Canadian Armies, and intensive air activity designed to pin the enemy down, 2SS Panzer Division had been concentrated on the American front, around St Eny, and almost daily, newly arrived infantry divisions were being identified along the US front. 272 and 276 Divisions had arrived from the south of France, and from Brittany and the Biscay areas, 5 Para., 276 and 353 Divisions moved to Normandy, together with 326 Division from north of the Seine. By 15 July, 1SS, 2SS, 21 and Lehr Panzer Divisions had been withdrawn into reserve, and only the timely intervention of GOODWOOD prevented their transfer to Bradley's sector. As it was, Panzer Lehr was the only heavy armour group transferred to the western sector.

First US Army continued its inevitably slow and frustrating advance south to the break-out start line. It is difficult indeed to depict the soggy battle-scarred terrain across which the American troops had to operate. The German formations fought with stubborn determination, but little by little were forced to yield ground until, on 17 July, Bradley's army was formed up on the line Lessay–Périers–St-Lô.

Moving in
Grim reminders of the recent bitter fighting litter a narrow lane as American troops prepare for the final assault on the town of St. Lo.

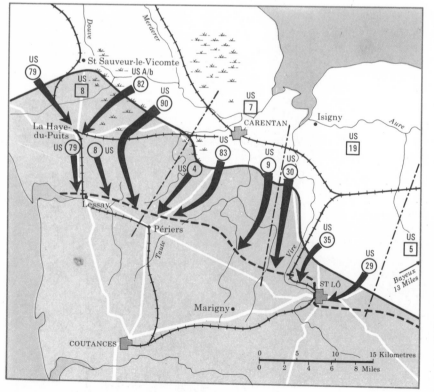

The American line-up : 3–18 July

————	Front line 3 July
– – – –	Front line 18 July
☐	Corps
○	Division

Additional hazard
American army Jeeps make their way through the flooded streets of a small town west of St. Lo after the banks of a nearby river had been blown by retreating German defenders.

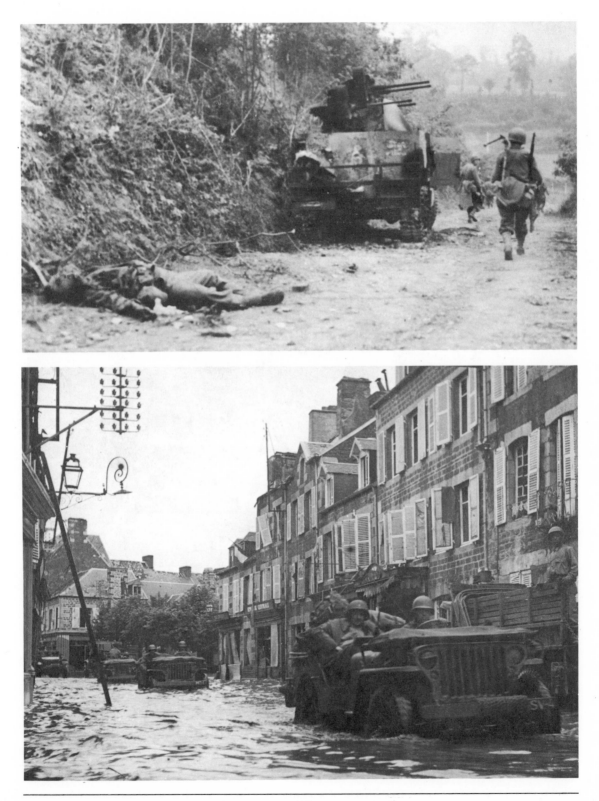

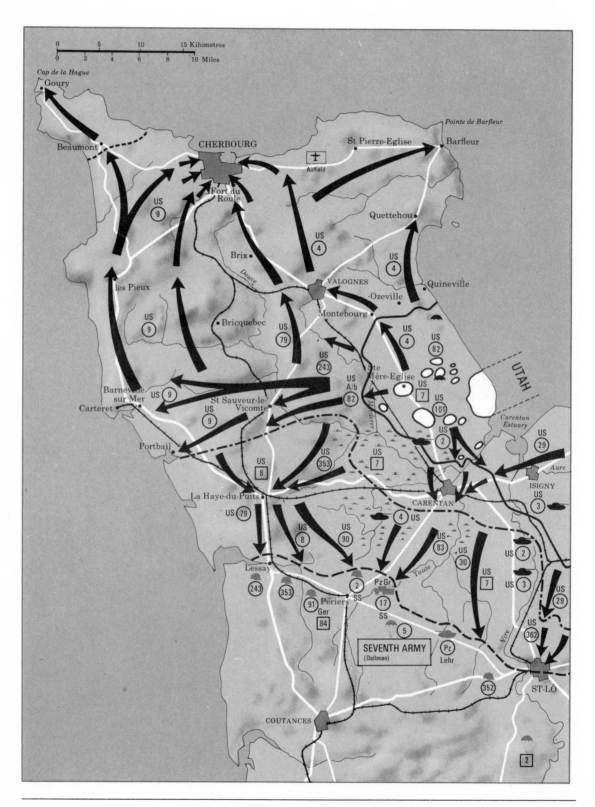

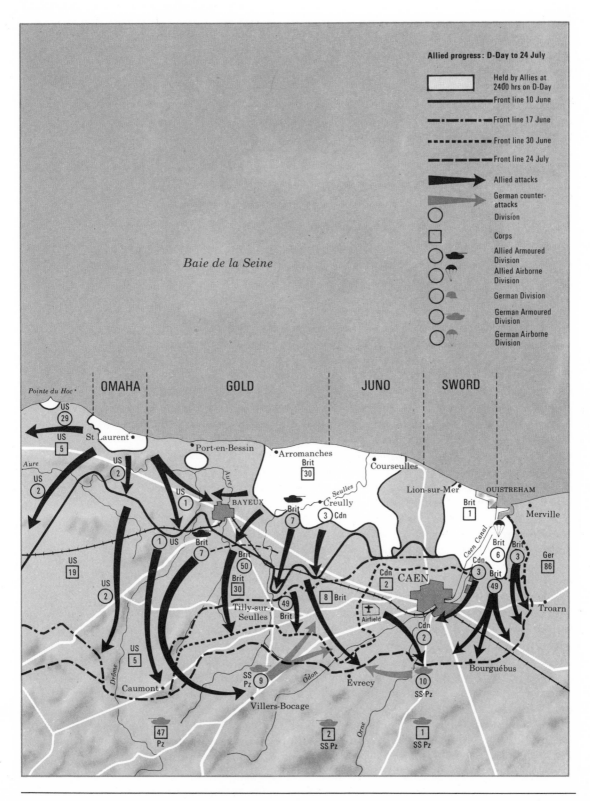

BREAK-OUT ON THE WESTERN FLANK: 25 JULY

At last General Bradley was ready to go. The initial assault, under the command of General Lawton Collins, 7 US Corps, was to be on a frontage of three infantry divisions. Having crossed the St-Lô–Périers road, these divisions were to thrust to a line from Marigny to St-Gilles, and then face outwards to establish the flanks of a corridor along which two armoured divisions and one infantry division were to advance – on the west at Coutances, and on the east to Canisy, and thence to Fervanches. 7 US Corps was to be followed by 8 US Corps of five divisions on the coastal sector, while 19 US Corps, backed up by 5 US Corps, was to strike towards Vire on the left flank.

The initial break-out assault on 25 July was preceded by a devastating air bombing offensive, which left many of the defending formations stunned – their heavier weapons wrecked and their field communications out of action. When the leading wave of ground troops went into action, pockets of fierce opposition were encountered, particularly in the western part of the break-out area, but resistance to the central column of the advance was light.

On 27 July, the decisive actions took place. Enemy formations along the entire front began to withdraw in the face of the onslaught. COBRA´ had achieved its first objective: the German front was broken and First US Army was on its way south. To assist the momentum of the break-out, 2 Canadian Corps attacked yet again towards the main Caen–Falaise road. The reaction was staunch and immediate. 1SS, 9SS, 12SS and 21 Panzer Divisions, backed by a strong gun-line of 88mm field-pieces, killed the Canadian offensive – but the turning point had been reached in the west. The American column was forcing its way south and the whole Allied front was beginning to pivot around Caumont.

Satisfied that the American break-out operation had succeeded, Montgomery's preoccupation was to continue to direct the British and Canadian Armies in a manner which would facilitate the *speed* of the American advance: speed being the essential factor if an encirclement was to be possible.

There remained six Panzer divisions east of Noyers, mainly grouped round Caen. West of Noyers there were no enemy armoured formations nearer than Panzer Lehr, located west of St-Lô. Montgomery decided to take advantage of this situation and ordered a thrust by 8 British Corps southwards towards Vire. Six divisions were to be involved: the remaining British and Canadian divisions were ordered to mount limited offensive actions to pin down the enemy confronting them.

The American thrust southwards carried all before it. By 31 July Granville and Avranches were captured and on 1 August, General Patton's HQ Third US Army became operational, initially taking command of 8 US Corps.

The break-out: 25 July

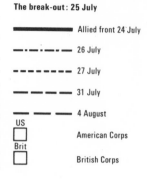

▬▬▬▬▬	Allied front 24 July
─·─·─·─	26 July
─ ─ ─ ─	27 July
─ ─ ─ ─	31 July
─ ─ ─	4 August
US ☐	American Corps
Brit ☐	British Corps

German dispositions: 25 July

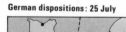

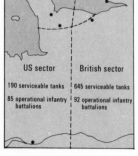

US sector	British sector
190 serviceable tanks	645 serviceable tanks
85 operational infantry battalions	92 operational infantry battalions

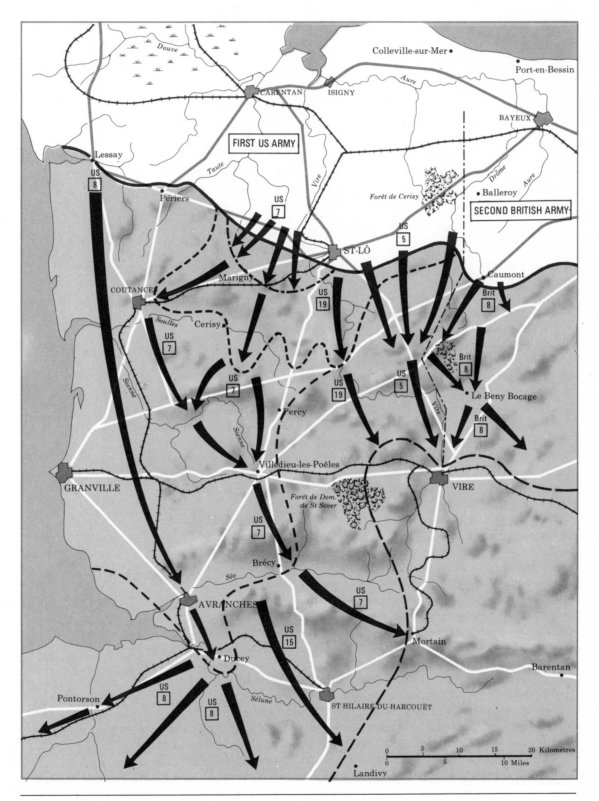

By 1 August, German Seventh Army was 'wet-henning' – that is, plugging holes in its line, and having to split formations into battle groups to make this possible. Four Panzer divisions, 1SS, 9SS, 10SS and 12SS, were left in the sector south of Caen, with 346, 272, 271 and 277 Infantry Divisions. 21 Panzer Division had been moved to the area south of Caumont, and to face the American break-out there remained only 2, 2SS and 116, together with what was left of Panzer Lehr. Of infantry divisions there remained only 17SS Panzer-Grenadier, 243 and 353, and apart from 353, all were by this time low in strength after the losses they had sustained.

Characteristically, General Patton 'had the whip out' and his Third US Army stormed south to reach Vannes on the south coast of Brittany on 5 August. Nantes, at the mouth of the River Loire, was occupied on the following day.

By 5 August it was clear that the enemy had failed in every attempt to form a co-ordinated front against the American advance southwards. It is necessary to take into account that most of the enemy divisions had been fighting without respite for nearly two months; that they had received little or no Luftwaffe protection from the unremitting attacks by the tactical air forces during the day, nor from heavy night bombing within the combat area or on its periphery. Moreover, their lines of communication were insecure from air attack, so that they suffered constantly from shortages of vehicle fuel, ammunition and every other logistical requirement.

I think that professional soldiers, and indeed anyone who can, for a moment, put aside political and other emotions stirred inevitably by the war with Germany, must express a profound respect for the German officers and men who fought with such courage and determination in such unpropitious conditions. During the crucial period

Gen. George Patton
Under Patton's forceful command, Third U.S. Army poured through the gap in the German lines created by Gen. Lawton Collins' initial breakout offensive, to reach the south coast of Brittany on 5 August. Loved by many, including the American press, but a thorn in the flesh of many senior Allied commanders, Patton was without doubt the most difficult field commander Eisenhower ever had to try to handle.

5–8 August, Montgomery repeatedly told me that he could not guess what German policy might be in the face of the break-out. On 8 August the enemy was still fighting desperately on a general line from Mortain to Vire, and thence on the River Orne south of Caen. General Patton's forward troops were near Le Mans and there was no enemy to prevent him from moving north on Alençon: his only problem was a shortage of vehicle fuel caused largely by the speed of his own advance. First Canadian Army, which by now had the Polish Armoured Division under command, was attacking successfully towards Falaise, and the Poles had also established a bridgehead over the River Dives.

With General Patton's army progressing eastwards on their southern flank, and thus denying them access to the River Loire, and with the British and Canadian armies already threatening their east-west communications between Argentan and Vire, the very obvious course for the German Seventh Army was to make a staged withdrawal to the River Seine. Montgomery thought that they would first pull back to the line of the River Orne, and thence cover the Seine west of Paris while ferries and floating bridges were prepared for their retreat.

The enemy was being compressed into a narrow salient, with its western front on the line Vire–Mortain subjected to remorseless attacks from all sides. He would inevitably have to pull back. But when? In what direction? And with what objective?

Montgomery's Orders: 6 August

As there was still no clear indication of how the German High Command was going to react to the rapidly worsening situation, Montgomery's decision was that the Allied forces should continue with plans to drive the enemy against the Seine. We were told at the same time that provision should be made to have on call an airborne division ready to be dropped in the Chartres gap in order to prevent the retreating enemy from escaping that way.

First Canadian Army was ordered to accelerate the capture of Falaise, whence its axis to the Seine would be along the line Lisieux to Rouen. Second British Army would strike towards Mantes–Gassicourt, with its right flank on a line through Argentan and l'Aigle.

After discussion with General Bradley, it was agreed that 12 US Army Group, now comprising First US Army (General Hodges) and Third US Army (General Patton), would approach the Seine on a broad front. The main weight of the advance was to be on the right flank, which, on reaching the Seine, was to swing up towards Paris. The Army groups would also provide flank protection along the Loire.

By 6 August there had arrived in Normandy from Fifteenth Army, not only 116 reserve Panzer Division, but also 84, 89 and 363 Infantry

The field commanders
General George S. Patton, commanding Third U.S. Army, confers with General Omar Bradley, Senior Commander of the U.S. forces in France, and General Sir Bernard Montgomery, Deputy Commander of the Allied forces, after the successful breakout from the western flank. In attendance, standing in the background, is Maj.-Gen. David Belchem, Head of Montgomery's Operations and Planning Staff.

Divisions, together with part of 6 Parachute Division. It was known that other formations were on the way from the north. At long last Hitler must have abandoned his conviction that Normandy was a diversion. That he would eventually reach this conclusion was obvious; what is remarkable is that the Allied Deception Plan had achieved such incredible success. For nearly two months, Fifteenth German Army had been idly standing by while Seventh Army was being driven to the wall. Although the reserve Panzer divisions had progressively been filtered south of the Seine, Seventh Army had been denied the infantry divisions which, by holding the front, would have allowed the armour to be concentrated for counter-attacks against the Allies.

Professionally, it must be added that this tactical and strategic failure was not the fault of the German generals. It was due solely to the intervention of Hitler, whose knowledge of the military profession was limited to 'intuitions' and a favourable horoscope.

German High Command
Photographed at a senior command meeting in Paris are, from left to right: Sperrle, Blasko-witz, Rommel, Speidel, Von Schweppenburg, and Plocher.

The Mortain Counter-attack

Of all Hitler's unmilitary decisions, perhaps the most incomprehensible was the way in which the newly arrived divisions were being thrown piecemeal into the Normandy battle when any experienced commander would have ordered them to be deployed into a firm base, towards which the sorely tried Seventh Army divisions could stage an orderly withdrawal – there to regroup, absorb reinforcements and prepare for a new offensive.

The period of uncertainty was short-lived. Totally disregarding the advice of his generals, and probably ignorant of the true situation on the front, Hitler personally ordered that the Panzer divisions should be concentrated outside Mortain, and from there launch a crushing blow due west between the rivers Sélune and Sée, to Avranches on the coast. His reasoning was that this attack would cut off General Patton's Third Army and cordon First US Army in the north. The Order of the Day issued to Seventh German Army stated that upon the operation ordered by the Führer depended the decision of the war in the west, 'and with it perhaps the decision of the war itself'.

In spite of all past experience, Hitler still did not understand that major offensive operations in war could not (in the mid 1940s) be undertaken without – at the very least – local air superiority over the battlefield. To make matters worse, the German High Command was being obliged to throw against the Allies its depleted, utterly tired and dispirited armoured forces, lacking in petrol and replacement stores. And this was at a juncture in the campaign when any experienced general would have re-formed his army on a strictly defensive deployment, on ground of his own choosing, in order to obtain a respite for his men and a chance to stock up for his next move. The German generals were, of course, fully aware that the Mortain counter-attack was a suicidal risk. But there was another factor of which they may not have been aware, and which left no opportunity for arguing with the Führer.

Field-Marshal Von Kluge
Despite his certain professional conviction that it could end only in total disaster, Von Kluge had no option but to act on the Fuhrer's orders and launch the doomed counter-attack on Mortain.

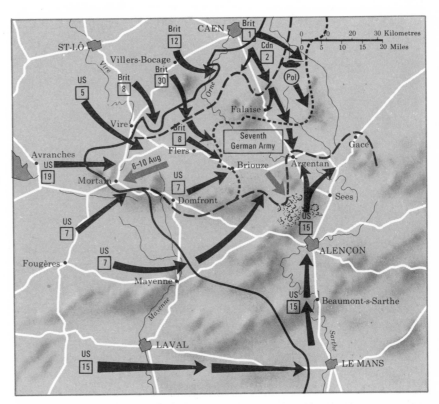

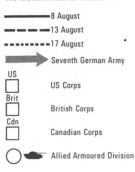

The Mortain counter-attack

- ———— 8 August
- – – – – 13 August
- ········· 17 August
- ➡ Seventh German Army

US □ US Corps

Brit □ British Corps

Cdn □ Canadian Corps

◯ 🛆 Allied Armoured Division

General Von Rundstedt had been replaced by Field-Marshal Von Kluge at the end of June. Von Kluge had been a favourite of Hitler's, but was not as loyal as the Führer believed. He had wavered between sympathy with the anti-Nazi conspirators against Hitler and loyalty to his officer's oath. But one of the conspirators obtained proof that Von Kluge had – in 1944 – accepted a 'gratuity' from Hitler of £20,000, and threatened to reveal this if Von Kluge did not become a member of their group. From that time, Von Kluge was fearful of being betrayed to Hitler: for him, an order from the Führer was sacrosanct. The Mortain counter-attack had to go ahead: it was a *Führerbefehl*.

The counter-attack began on 7 August. The real strength of the German force is difficult to assess, because the formations were very depleted, but there were involved 1SS, 2, 2SS, 10SS and 116 Panzer Divisions and 84 and 363 Infantry Divisions. 30 US Division held the initial assault until two further American divisions in the area could be switched to the fight. The weather was ideal for air operations and the might of the Allied air forces was directed on the enemy advance. It is difficult to understand how the German troops withstood the intensive and continuous attacks brought to bear on them throughout the day. Their task was impossible: their losses were appalling. The American ground forces reacted in splendid fashion and the outcome of the battle was never in doubt. Hitler's desperate gamble had failed – and at a terrible price.

Bitter skirmish
*In the battle to take
Falaise a Sherman tank
pours cannon and machine
gun fire into shattered
buildings in support of
Canadian troops flushing
out German snipers.*

THE ENCIRCLEMENT

With the Mortain counter-attack so obviously doomed to failure, Montgomery's preoccupation was to accelerate the Allied thrust to the Seine, in keeping with his broad encirclement plan, meanwhile closing the Chartres gap. But Bradley suggested that the suicidal Mortain attack by the Germans offered an opportunity for an 'inner encirclement' of the enemy. If Third US Army could send a Corps north from Le Mans to Argentan and on towards Falaise, to meet 2 Canadian Corps and the Polish Armoured Division driving south, the German troops comprising the remnants of the Mortain counter-attack could be rounded up.

Montgomery agreed at once to Bradley's suggestion – but on one condition; and this was that Patton's army would not be delayed in its advance to the Seine. No general was more eager than Patton to take advantage of a 'straight run', but he was already frustrated by shortage of vehicle fuel, which had to be transported from the Normandy beaches on an indirect routing through Avranches. Accordingly his 15 US Corps was turned north from Le Mans to Argentan.

Closure of the Falaise Pocket

The gap was not, however, closed as quickly as had been intended. The Germans fought desperately to hold open an escape route to the east; and there were also problems with the closure plan which will no doubt be blamed on the British and American Operational Staffs. The spearheads of Third US Army and of 1 British Corps were approaching one another head-on, the former from the south, and the latter from the north. Our problem was to determine accurately at any given time the exact position of the leading troops on both sides.

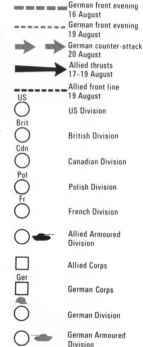

Closure of the Falaise Pocket: 16 to 20 August

German front evening 16 August

German front evening 19 August

German counter-attack 20 August

Allied thrusts 17–19 August

Allied front line 19 August

US — US Division

Brit — British Division

Cdn — Canadian Division

Pol — Polish Division

Fr — French Division

Allied Armoured Division

Allied Corps

Ger — German Corps

German Division

German Armoured Division

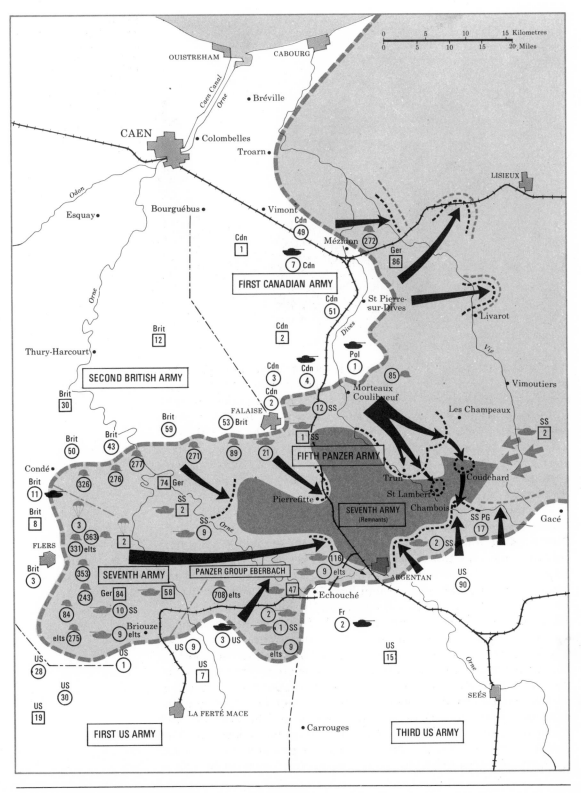

Falaise: 17 August
The photographs on these pages show the scene of complete devastation in Falaise as the Allied cordon tightened on the doomed town. Even the most battle-hardened of the Allied commanders were stunned by the scale of the death and destruction revealed in the mopping up operation.

We then had to advise the various air forces of the bomb-line, so that they in turn could brief their pilots where it was safe to attack. Secondly we had to pass the maximum and minimum range information to the artillery on both sides for the same reason, and these requirements took time to disseminate through the normal radio networks. Perhaps we were over-cautious; but the political repercussions, had we bombed our Allies or been bombed by them, were risks we declined to accept. To avoid unnecessary risks it was decided that Patton would halt his advance at Argentan.

The stubborn Falaise pocket was finally closed on 19 August, when American troops driving from the south towards Chambois met 4 Canadian Armoured and the Polish Armoured Divisions converging on the town from the northwest and northeast. As the noose tightened, this tiny area of Normandy contained the shattered remnants of some eighteen German army formations. The battle for Falaise lasted for nearly two weeks. Initially the beleaguered enemy retained some degree of organization – the infantry units fighting in the west while the remnants of the Panzer Divisions battled desperately to keep open a narrow escape route at the neck: but by 16 August the situation was chaotic. For some time after 19 August, the Allied formations were fully occupied in rounding up the dispersed groups of confused enemy survivors – each group containing, perhaps, members of up to a dozen different units. The wreckage and confusion within the 'pocket' is difficult to describe: enemy transport vehicles, guns and tanks were found packed nose to tail in a landscape of total devastation.

The Allied Drive to the Seine

The fact that Third US Army did not advance north of Argentan proved to our advantage. General Patton's army at last received vehicle fuel replenishment and his 5, 15 and 19 US Corps raced ahead to the Seine without becoming involved in the final stages of closing the Falaise gap. US Third Army, without German opposition, passed through Dreux and Chartres on 15 August, and through Orleans on the following day. Because First US Army and the Commonwealth Armies had been delayed in clearing up the appalling mess in the Falaise pocket, and in opening routes to facilitate their own advance eastwards, Montgomery ordered Bradley to reach the Seine and thence to advance westwards along the south bank of the river in order to prevent any escaping Germans from crossing the river, pending the arrival of 21 Army Group.

The Seine bridges had been destroyed by air action, but, on arrival at Mantes-Gassicourt, the leading American units found a catwalk across the river, used by the sluice-gate operators. The first Allied crossing of the Seine was made by a single file of soldiers. There were no enemy troops on the far bank. It was D + 75.

The Allied drive to the Seine

Corps thrusts

US — American Corps

Brit — British Corps

Cdn — Canadian Corps

Meanwhile, Montgomery urged the Canadian Army to hasten its advance through Lisieux to the Seine, and ordered 6 Airborne Division and 51 Division to be more aggressive in their thrust to the east. It must be borne in mind that on the east flank of the Allied bridgehead there remained operational those German divisions which had not been involved in the Mortain counter-attack; they included the 85, 272, 331, 346, 711 Infantry Divisions, with a part of 12SS Panzer Division. Behind them were 17 GAF, 344 and 348 Infantry, and 6 Parachute Divisions. Eight of these formations had been belatedly switched to Normandy from the German Fifteenth Army north of the Seine. 21 Army Group had to drive these forces eastwards to the river, while Patton's forces moved forward behind them reaching as far as Elboeuf, Henderbonville and Vernon.

As the British and Canadian units came forward, Patton's troops pulled back to their sector, and the Allies got sorted out while General Leclerc's French Armoured Division proudly entered Paris. Patton meanwhile had secured an undamaged bridge at Melun, east of the capital.

There is no reliable record of how many German survivors succeeded in crossing to the north of the Seine. Some histories speak of 60 ferries plying across the river between Elboeuf and Le Havre together, no doubt, with some boats and rafts. But since the diminishing area available was subjected to air attack by day and by night, the number who escaped cannot have been significant.

By the end of August, all four Allied armies were across the Seine and Montgomery handed over direct day-to-day tactical direction of the battle to Eisenhower. A new phase began in the Allied thrust towards the heart of Germany.

The Seine crossings
German machine-gun fire rakes the water perilously close to a group of U.S. Army engineers ferrying a vehicle over the river on pontoons.

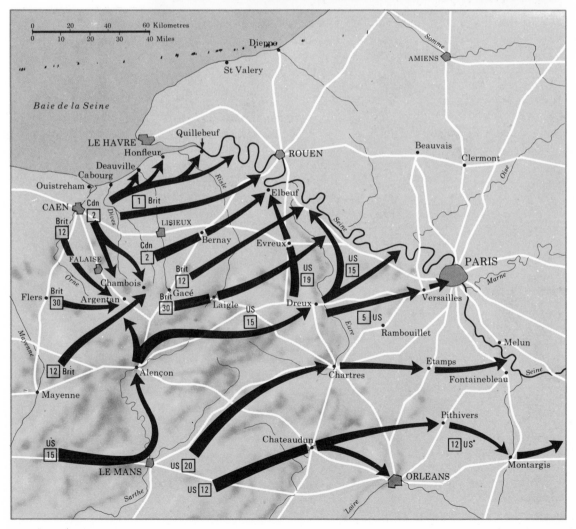

PART VII

Perspective on Normandy

A REVIEW OF THE BATTLE FOR NORMANDY

That the Allied success in Normandy was so much greater than could ever have been foreseen, was due primarily to the weaknesses in German strategy. Hitler's personal intervention in the direction of the battle, despite the professional advice of his generals, provided the Allies with opportunities which they were not slow to exploit. When the only sound course open to the German Army at the end of July was to withdraw behind the Seine and Loire in an attempt to contain the invasion in northwestern France, the Führer sought to fight it out in Normandy. As a result, he suffered a staggering defeat. In manpower, the German losses were roughly half a million men; 240,000 killed or wounded, and 210,000 taken prisoner. Material losses were equally severe. They included 3,500 pieces of artillery; some 1,500 tanks; a vast quantity of motor and horse transport, and countless tons of equipment of all kinds. More than 43 entire divisions had been eliminated or reduced to cadres.

A Triumph of Forward Planning

It has been shown that the battle was fought as planned before we left London in June although, inevitably, some delays and setbacks were imposed on the Allies by the changing course of the operations and, even more so, by the incidence of adverse weather conditions in June and July. The battle ended German domination of France, and had repercussions throughout the world in inspiring confidence in the power of the Western Allied armies to overcome the Wehrmacht.

Throughout the Normandy campaign the basic principle of our strategy was to attract and retain the main enemy strength on our eastern flank in order to facilitate a break-out on the western flank, and there to exploit the American competence in extremely rapid mobility in order to encircle the enemy forces. The extent to which this succeeded is well illustrated by the following table, which shows the distribution of enemy forces on the Allied front during June and July 1944.

1944	Opposite the US Sector: Cherbourg Peninsula to (but excluding) Caumont			Opposite the British Sector: Caumont to the Caen Area		
	Panzer Divisions	Serviceable Tanks	Infantry Battalions	Panzer Divisions	Serviceable Tanks	Infantry Battalions
June 15	–	70	63	4	520	43
June 30	½	140	63	7½	725	64
July 10	2	190	72	6	610	65
July 20	3	190	82	5	560	71
July 25	2	190	85	6	645	92

The end of an army
German coastal defence troops surrender under the initial onslaught on UTAH beach. By the end of the Normandy battle, Hitler's Seventh Army had been destroyed, with 240,000 men killed or wounded and 210,000 taken prisoner.

At no time were the Allies forced to conform to enemy thrusts designed to undermine our 'balance' on the battlefield, or to distort the concept of the original master plan. By contrast the Germans *were* forced to commit their reserves in a piecemeal fashion, and this precluded the concentration of a mass of armour competent to make a clear breach in our dispositions with a resultant disruption of our strategic and tactical plans.

The most important result of the Normandy battle in the longer term was that the Allied armies lined up on the River Seine some 39 divisions strong, starting on D+75, when General Patton crossed the river at Mantes-Gassicourt. All arrived within the D+90 limit which Montgomery had set as his goal in London, and the current appreciation of the German capabilities in Western Europe at that time suggested that the enemy's power of resistance in the theatre of operations was on the verge of collapse. Northwest of the Ardennes, in Belgium and Holland, there were elements of two Panzer divisions and nine infantry divisions, all in full retreat. South of the Ardennes there were two Panzer Grenadier divisions and four very depleted infantry divisions. In the Rhône valley, the diversion of the Allied forces which had landed in the south of France was driving before it half a Panzer division and two infantry divisions.

In such circumstances, it was obvious that Hitler would have to produce additional divisions – from Germany (where our intelligence indicated that he had none available); from other fronts (in the east) or from Italy – if he was to prevent an Allied thrust towards the Reich. The dependence of the German war effort on the Ruhr industrial region (to the extent of 50 per cent of the crude steel and 52 per cent of the hard coal) suggested that Hitler would concentrate most of his resources in the north – an appreciation reinforced by his known preoccupation with the V1 rocket sites in the Pas de Calais.

When Montgomery handed over the command of the Allied forces to Eisenhower at the Seine, the main problem was to decide how best to take advantage of the situation in order to finish the war in the west as quickly as possible. It was obvious, at that time, that one powerful, highly concentrated thrust from the Seine could not fail to reach the Rhine.

Inter-services Co-operation

The victory of the ground forces in Normandy could not have been achieved without the total, and remarkably successful, co-operation which existed between the naval, merchant navy, air and army services.

First consideration must be given to the Allied air forces. They played an important part in the winning of the Battle of the Atlantic. Above all, by early 1944, they had established mastery in the air over Europe. It is no reflection on the parts played by the Navy and the Army to state that they could not have hoped to achieve such splendid results had they not been assured of constant overhead cover. The role of the Allied air forces in the invasion exercise began long before June 1944. Their long-range tasks included attacks on German oil refineries, air bases and Luftwaffe installations; the interdiction programme was of tremendous importance in restricting the German forces' ability to reinforce and supply their troops in Normandy; the fighter cover and coastal command activities made possible the assembly and movement of shipping in the English Channel virtually without Luftwaffe interference; the tactical air forces' attacks on enemy movements, and fighter protection against Luftwaffe interference, were a direct participation in the battle of primary importance, and the fact that our own troops were visually aware of the air forces' protection above them greatly contributed to their confidence and morale.

The Allied navies are normally accustomed to rate victory in terms of the number of enemy ships sunk or damaged. But in the annals of the Royal Navy, the United States Navy and the Merchant Navy, Normandy will assuredly rank as one of the most skilfully planned and executed operations in naval history. The magnitude of the organizational problem may be judged by the cross-channel movements, which involved some 7,000 craft of all types, from battleships to the smallest categories of landing craft. The operational sea-going tasks included the protection of the vital sea lanes from attacks by German U-boats and surface torpedo craft. The organization of minor craft and merchant ships in the lanes cleared (and then kept cleared) of mines, needs no emphasis. But because these roles were so successfully accomplished, little mention is made of them in most accounts of the invasion. Above all, the contribution of naval gunfire, in the assault phase particularly, was of crucial importance. The intended blanketing of the coastal artillery of the Atlantic Wall by massed air bombardment failed to a large extent, and units of the Allied navies provided essential fire-support in getting the assault troops ashore. This was apparent, in different ways, on all five of the assault beaches, but perhaps above all on OMAHA, where eight destroyers risked running aground in order to provide the vital support fire without which the landing might well have failed.

Mention has already been made of the naval gunfire support in the operations to establish and maintain the bridgehead, and the battleships, monitors and cruisers continued to provide this until the end of June. Perhaps the climax of the naval bombardment came on the night of 12–13 June, when HMS *Ramillies* and HMS *Nelson* hit Caen with a 15-inch or 16-inch shell every 30 seconds.

It is particularly appropriate here to record the achievements of the Merchant Navy in handling the sea transit of personnel and stores during the landing period. Statistics are available covering the period 6 June to 31 August, when the totals involved were:

	American	British
Men	1,220,000	830,000
Vehicles	236,000	203,000
Stores (tonnes)	1,850,000	1,240,000

In the background of the seaborne transit system was a 'Build-Up Control Organization', which experience in the Mediterranean had proved essential. According to the run of the battle, the priority of stores urgently required in Normandy altered. In military language we speak of an 'artillery battle', when the primary requirement tends to be gun ammunition, and of a 'mobile battle', when the call is for vehicle fuel and associated stores.

The Build-Up Control Organization has to decide on loading priorities for the supply ships and provide for the necessary dispatch and handling of the appropriate stores in a logistical supply chain which may reach right back to the point of manufacture. An interesting example of the detailed planning involved in this task arose in connection with ammunition deliveries to the warships in the invasion battle. Normally the preponderance of warship ammunition is 'armour-piercing', designed to penetrate hostile warships. But for operations in support of ground troops, high-explosive (fragmentary) rounds were required. The change-over involved unloading A.P. rounds from the ships and returning them to store in the UK, and at the same time procuring H.E. missiles from appropriate depots in Britain, arranging transit to the selected port, and then shipping them to the appropriate warship.

The destruction of the American 'Mulberry' off St-Laurent produced many arguments about the value of these artificial harbours. What is quite certain is that the Gooseberry breakwaters were of inestimable value – all the time, and not purely during the great storm. The Mulberry piers were criticized because eventually, in the St-Laurent sector, the Americans were landing more per day across open beaches than was the case at Arromanches, where the British harbour was repaired and utilized. The concensus of opinion seems to be that both alternatives were justified. The problems on the American beach were solved by the introduction of a whole range of new unloading techniques. American initiative and technological experience were brought to bear and characteristically resolved the difficulties. On the British side, the Mulberry did provide certain facilities for off-loading difficult and 'awkward' loads, which caused the Americans much more time and effort.

During the period up to the end of August the losses sustained by the Allied forces were grievous indeed. But it is some consolation to record that, bearing in mind the task of breaking through the much vaunted Atlantic Wall, they were considerably lower than had been feared.

	Total Manpower Involved	Losses (killed, wounded and missing)
US Forces	1,220,000	126,000
British and Canadian Forces	830,000	84,000

The Opposing Forces

It must be borne in mind that the German forces at divisional and lower levels fought with great skill and tenacity. This would be expected in the case of élite troops of the SS formations, but in fact it applied to virtually all the Panzer and infantry divisions, among which I have mentioned 352 German Division as an example, because of personal experience. Our soldiers were faced by high-calibre troops.

In this context, our principal 'ally' was Hitler. Our problems would have been immeasurably greater if he had not interfered in the direction of his forces, in spite of the advice and opinions of the German generals who were for the most part professionally competent. There can be little doubt that had the direction of operations in Normandy been left to the German field commanders, the Allies might well have found themselves enclosed in the Normandy Deployment Zone, faced by a powerful and well co-ordinated enemy cordon. The subsequent breakout from the western flank would then have posed enormous problems and the eventual Allied advance through France and beyond to the borders of Germany would have been bitterly contested, step by step. Even if forced to retreat, the German armies would have been able to do so in an orderly and controlled manner and fierce resistance would have been offered on each of the major river barriers – the Marne, Meuse, Moselle and Rhine – which lay across the line of the Allied advance.

There is only one major aspect of war in which some of the German commanders lacked experience, and this was in the understanding of the tremendous importance of tactical air power. Rommel understood this because of his experience in fighting the Allies in North Africa. But the others, who had fighting experience in France and on the Soviet front, had not wholly appreciated that in the mid-1940s, offensive operations deprived of at least local air superiority could not succeed. It is no wonder that the Führer had no conception of this vital factor.

Postscript

But perhaps the greatest significance of the overwhelming victory in Normandy is that when the Allied armies lined up along the River Seine, General Eisenhower was offered a fleeting opportunity to launch a concentrated thrust right through to the River Rhine, whence the Ruhr industrial region could have been encircled and the war in the west successfully terminated by the end of 1944.

But that is another story.

The Battlefield Memorials

The Commonwealth War Graves Commission, established by Royal Charter in 1917, and the American Battle Monuments Commission, established just a few years later, are both founded on the fundamental principle that every one of the thousands of men and women who died in the military service of their country should be commemorated – permanently, individually, and by name – no matter where in the world they died.

Nor was any distinction to be made on the grounds of military, civil or social rank. The graves of the known dead are marked by row upon row of simple uniform white crosses or headstones, while the names of those whose bodies were never recovered, or who died at sea, are engraved on permanent commemorative monuments or on walls of remembrance.

For those who might wish to visit the grave of a relative, or simply see for themselves the peaceful shoreline and countryside that was once the scene of such bitter conflict, these maps show the location of the main cemeteries and memorials: more detailed information will be found on the following pages.

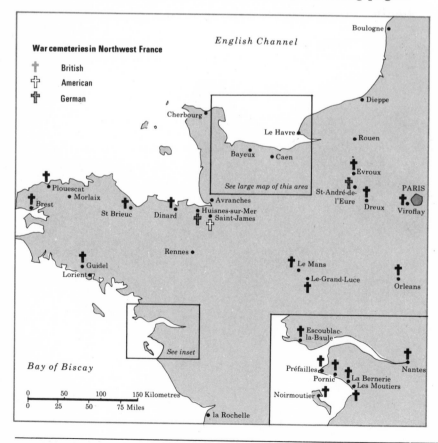

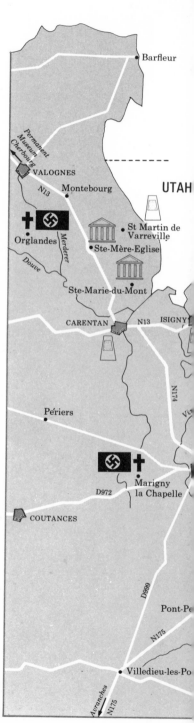

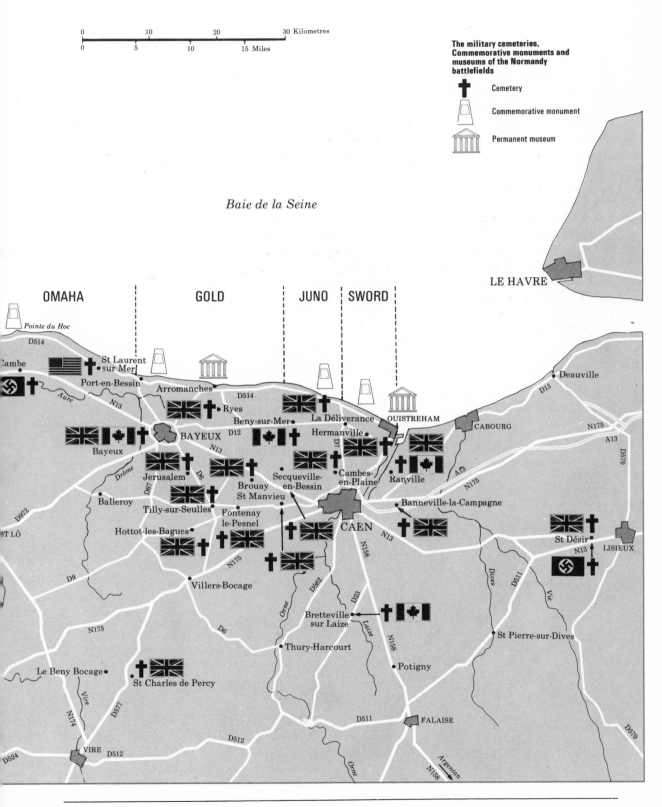

0   10   20   30 Kilometres

0   5   10   15 Miles

The military cemeteries, Commemorative monuments and museums of the Normandy battlefields

Cemetery

Commemorative monument

Permanent museum

Baie de la Seine

LE HAVRE

OMAHA   GOLD   JUNO   SWORD

Pointe du Hoc

D514

Cambe

St Laurent sur Mer

Port-en-Bessin

Arromanches

D514

Deauville

D13

Ryes

Beny-sur-Mer

La Déliverance

OUISTREHAM

D514

Hermanville

CABOURG

N175

A13

D579

BAYEUX

D12

Bayeux

N13

Secqueville-en-Bessin

Cambes-en-Plaine

Ranville

Banneville-la-Campagne

A13

N175

Jerusalem

Brouay

St Manvieu

Drôme

D6

D67

Balleroy

Tilly-sur-Seulles

Fontenay le-Pesnel

CAEN

N13

St Désir

LISIEUX

Hottot-les-Bagues

D972

ST LÔ

N175

D9

Villers-Bocage

D562

D23

N158

Orne

Bretteville sur Laize

Laize

N158

St Pierre-sur-Dives

Le Beny Bocage

St Charles de Percy

Vire

D577

Thury-Harcourt

Potigny

Dives

D511

Vie

D579

N175

D6

N174

VIRE

D524

D512

D512

D511

FALAISE

Orne

Argentan

N158

Beny-sur-Mer
*More than two thousand
Canadian servicemen are
buried at Beny-sur-Mer,
just a short way inland
from the D-Day beaches.
The simple layout of
the graves, the borders
of shrubs and flowers,
the Cross of Sacrifice
and the terrace bearing
the memorial tablets to
those whose bodies were
never recovered, or who
were cremated, follows a
pattern adopted by the
allied nations for all their
war cemeteries.*

'Known unto God'
*A simple inscription
tells all that is known
of the soldier buried
beneath this headstone.
His name will be one of
the many listed on the
memorial monument as
having no known grave.*

Making enquiries

In addition to their major work of establishing and maintaining military cemeteries and memorials throughout the world, both the Commonwealth War Graves Commission and the American Battle Monuments Commission are able, and only too willing, to extend their help to any member of the public wishing to discover the whereabouts of the grave or memorial of a relative or friend.

Enquirers should write to one of the addresses given below and should include as much information as possible about the casualty-his full name, rank and number; his unit; his age, and town of birth; and if possible the date and place of his death.

Commonwealth
The Enquiries Office
Commonwealth War Graves Commission
2, Marlow Road
Maidenhead
Berkshire SL6 7DX

American
American Battle Monuments Commission
4C014 Forrestal Building
1000, Independence Avenue, S.W.
Washington, D.C. 20314

or to the European office at:
68, rue du 19 Janvier
92–Garches, France

The principal national cemeteries
Brief details are listed below of the twenty-seven military cemeteries in which are buried, or commemorated, most of the Allied and German troops who were killed in the Normandy battles. It should, however, be remembered that in addition to the thousands of graves in these official cemeteries, many hundreds more serving men of all armies were buried in small military plots in local church graveyards near to where they fell in battle.

American
St. Laurent-sur-Mer, the main American cemetery in Normandy, situated overlooking OMAHA Beach between Arromanches and Grandcamp. Contains 9,386 graves.

St. James, the main American cemetery in Brittany, lies just outside the village of St. James, about twelve miles south of Avranches. Contains 4,410 graves.

British
Banneville-Sannerville, situated between Caen and Troarn. Contains 2,175 graves.

Bayeux, largest of the British and Commonwealth cemeteries. Contains 3,934 graves.
Brouay, between Caen and Bayeux. Contains 377 graves.
Cambes-en-Plaine, located between Caen and Courseulles. Contains 224 graves.
Chouain (Jerusalem), between Bayeux and Tilly-sur-Seulles. Contains 40 graves.
Douvres-la-Delivrande, between Caen and Luc-sur-Mer. Contains 927 graves.
Fontenay-le-Pesnel, situated between Caen and Caumont-l'Eventé. Contains 520 graves.
Hermanville-sur-Mer, on the coast. Contains 986 graves.
Hottot-les-Bagues, between Caen and Caumont-l'Eventé. Contains 965 graves.
Ranville, situated close to 'Pegasus' bridge. Contains 2,151 graves.
Ryes, between Bayeux and Arromanches. Contains 630 graves.
Saint-Manvieu, situated between Caen and Caumont. Contains 2,186 graves.
Secqueville-en-Bessin, between Caen and Bayeux. Contains 117 graves.
Tilly-sur-Seulles, located between Caen and Balleroy. Contains 1,224 graves.
Saint-Charles-de-Percy, near Bény-Bocage. Contains 744 graves.
Saint-Desir-de-Lisieux, situated just outside Lisieux. Contains 569 graves.

Canadian
Beny-sur-Mer, located near Courseulles. Contains 2,043 graves.
Bretteville-sur-Laize, between Caen and Falaise. Contains 2,959 graves.

The cemeteries at **Bayeux** and **Ranville,** listed above, also contain the graves of many Canadian servicemen.

Polish
Grainville-Langannerie, between Caen and Falaise. Contains 650 graves.

German
La Cambe, situated between Bayeux and Isigny. Contains 21,160 graves.
Champigny-St-Andre-de-l'Eure. Contains 19,794 graves.
Huisnes-sur-Mer, near to Pontorson. Contains 11,956 graves.
Marigny-La-Chapelle-en-Juger. near St. Lô. Contains 11,169 graves.
Orglandes, near Valognes in the Cherbourg peninsula. Contains 10,152 graves.
Saint-Desir-de-Lisieux, outside Lisieux. Contains 3,635 graves.

The principal museums and monuments
For the convenience of the traveller exploring the coastal region of northwestern France, these additional places of interest are listed according their location within the designated D-Day beach landing areas.

UTAH
Military Museums at Ste-Mere-Eglise, Ste-Marie du Mont and Cherbourg. Commemorative monuments at Carentan, Ste-Mere-Eglise and St.-Martin-de-Varreville.

OMAHA
Commemorative monuments at St-Laurent-sur-Mer, Isigny-sur-Mer and Point-du-Hoe.

GOLD
The Liberation Memorial at Bayeux; Museum of the Normandy Landings at Arromanches; Commemorative memorial at Port-en-Bessin.

JUNO
Commemorative monument at Bernieres, and memorials at Courseulles and St-Aubin.

SWORD
Commemorative monument at Benouville; War Museums at Ouistreham-Riva-Bella and Benouville.

Index _____

Page numbers in Roman
type (46) refer to the
main text: page numbers
in Bold type (**46**) refer to
photographic illus-
strations and diagrams,
and their accompanying
captions.
Compiled by David
Wilson.

A

Aigle, 166
Air Forces, Review of
    Achievements, 180, 181
    Operations, 58–62, 74,
    83, 84, 114–5, 124, 127,
    142, 150, 154, 164, 169
    Command Structure, 63
    Reconnaissance, 62, 64
    RAF night sortie, **59**
    RAF tactical strike, **58**
    Typhoon rocket
    attacks on Armour,
    110, 111, 112
    see also Airborne
    Landings
Airborne Landings, 67–8,
    68, 74–83, **75**, **79**
Aircraft
    A–20 Havoc, **83**
    B–17 Flying Fortress, **61**
    Republic P–47, **19**
    Spitfire, **20**
    Typhoon, **110**
Airstrip requirements, 49,
    51–2
Allied Front, 10–18 July,
    152
    Plan of Campaign,
    42–55
    Progress, D-Day to
    24 July, 161 (map)
Audouville, 88
Argentan, 49, 51–2, 151,
    166, 170, 172, 174
Arromanches, 102, 104,
    140, 142, **143**, 182
Artillery, 116, 131, 132,
    150, 152, **164**
    see also Coastal
    Artillery
Assault Areas, 42–3
    (maps), 43
    Choice of, 20–5, 21
    (map), 42
    Deception Plan, 37
    German assessments,
    32–6
    see also Beach-heads
Atlantic Wall, 28–33,
    36–8, 60, 83, 90–1, 98–9,
    101, 119
Aunay, 138
Aure, River, 126
Avranches, 162, 168

B

Balleroy, 126
Barker, Brig.-Gen. R. W.,
    10
Barneville-sur-Mer, 130,
    138
Barry, Rear-Adm., **128**
Bayeux, 95, 104, 119, 120,
    126
Beach Defences, 28, **28**,
    32, 93, 96, 100 (map),
    106–7
    see also Coastal Defences
Beach-heads, 44–5, 118–21
    see also under specific
    names, *e.g.* Utah
Bedell-Smith, Lt. Gen.,
    12, **12**, 64
Belchem, Maj. Gen.
    David, 128, **167**
Belgian 1 Infantry
    Brigade, 68
Bénouville Bridge, 110,
    112
Bernieres-sur-Mer, 106–7
Biéville, 110, 112
Biscay, Bay of, 32, 50
Blaskowitz, Gen., 28,
    168
Blay, 128
Bocage, 24, **25**, 49, **76**, 78,
    139, 144
Bodyguard *see* Operation
    Bodyguard
Bourgébus, 154, 157
Bradley, Lt. Gen. Omar,
    12, 54, **54**, 66, 68, 124,
    136, **148**, 149, 152, 154,
    155, 156, 157, 167, 170,
    174
Breakout from Bridge-
    head, 148–75
    Preparations, 148–61
    Breakout on Western
    Flank, 162–9, 162–3
    (maps)
    Encirclement, 170–5
Breakwaters, 15–6, 69,
    140, 143, 181–2
Bricquebec, 137
Bridges, 48, 49, 58–60,
    74–6, 125, 127, 130, 149,
    174
Bridgehead, 114–5 (maps),
    119, 122–45, 133, 145
    Establishment, 7–12
    June, 124–9
    Development, 13–19
    June, 130–5
    Establishment of Odon
    138–9
British Army
    2nd Army, 43, 43 (map)
    47, 52, 66–7, 68, 124,
    131, 132, 136, 139, 140,
    142, 148, 149, 150, 151,
    152, 166
    Corps
        1: 99, 105, 132, 143,
        170

8: 131, 132, 138, 139,
    142, 143
12: 152
30: 99, 104, 131, 138,
    139, 142, 143
Divisions
    Guards Armoured:
    154
    3 Infantry: 99, 105,
    108, 109–10, 120,
    124, 126, 132, 139,
    150
    6 Airborne: 68, 74–6,
    82, 105, 109, 110,
    112, **113**, 120, 126,
    130, 151, 174
    7 Armoured: 126, 131,
    138, 140, 154,
    11 Armoured: 131,
    132, 138, 140, 154
    15 Infantry: 132
    43 Infantry: 132, 152
    49 Infantry: 138, 150,
    152
    50 Infantry: 95, 99,
    100, 102, 1 4, 105,
    108, 119, 125, 126,
    152
    51 Highland: 131,
    132, 138, 139, 143,
    151, 174
    59 Infantry: 150
Brigades
    1 SAS: 109, 112
    8 Armoured: 126, 150
    9: 120
    see also Commando,
    SAS, Hussars, Royal
    Warwickshires *and*
    Shropshire Light In-
    fantry, Staffordshire
    Yeomanry
British Combined
    Services Committee, 10
British HQs, 128
    Siting, 134–5
Brittany, 49, 50, 136
Broadhurst, AVM Harry,
    68, 135
Brooke, Gen. Sir Alan, **128**
Build-Up Control Organ-
    ization, 181
Bulldozers, 93

C

Caen, 49–52, 55, **58**, 68,
    108, 110, 112, 120, 126,
    127, 131, 132, 138, 139,
    142, 143, 144, 145, 148
    By-pass Thrust, 153–7,
    151 (map)
    Fall of, 150, **150–1**, 151
    (map)
    Set-back, 140–5
Caen Canal, 74, 75 (map)
    105
Caen-Merville area, 75
    (map)
Calais, Pas de, 28, 34, 35,
    36, 56, 61, 127, 144, 179

Canadian Army
    1st Army: 68: 166, 174
    2nd Corps: 162, 170
    Divisions
        3: 99, 105, 106–7, 124,
        125, 126, 132· 139,
        150
        4 Armoured: 172
        9 Brigade: 107, 108
Canaris, Adm., 36
Canisy, 162, **164**
Carentan, 45, 46, **76**, 77,
    124, 130, 132, 137, 138,
    140, 142, 149
Carpiquet, 107–8, 150
Casualties
    D-Day, 118–9, **118**
    D-Day to Aug. 31: 182
    German, 137, **158**
    German Senior
    Command, 134
Caumont, 130, 132, 138,
    139, 140, 143, 149, 162
Cemeteries, 184–7, 184–5
    (maps), **187**
Chartres, 174
Chartres Gap, 144, 149,
    166, 170
Cherbourg Peninsula, 68,
    79, 80, 82, 119, 124, 127,
    130, 132, 143, 144, 160
    (map)
    Fall of, 136–8, **136**
    (map), 137
Cheux, 138
Churchill, Winston S.,
    10, **10**, 15, 66, **128**
Cicero, 36
Coastal Artillery, **22**, 28,
    30, **31**, **91**, **99**, **103**
Coastal Defences, 28–33,
    36–38, 60, 83, 90–1, 98–9,
    101, 119
Cobra *See* Operation
    Cobra
Colleville, 94, 108, 138
Collins, Gen. Lawton, 162
Colombelles, 152
Commando
    4: 108
    47: 100, 125
Conflict within Allied
    Command Structure
    44, 51–5, 68, 154, 156–7
Conningham, Air
    Marshal Sir Arthur, 68
COSSAC, 10, 12, 14, 42
Coutances, 162
Creully, 128

D

D-Day Assault, 72–121
    Air supremacy, 114–5,
    179
    Airborne landings,
    74-83
    Casualties, 118–9, **118**
    Date, 17, 62–4
    Detailed Plan, 66–71,
    66 (map)

German reaction, 78,
Naval Supremacy,
116–8
Order of Battle, **70–1**
Reflections, 114–20
Seaborne assault,
84–121, **85**
Statistics, 115–6
de Gaulle, Gen., **10**
Deception Plan, 33, 36,
56–7, **56–7**, 60–2, 114,
167
Decoy operations, 80–1
Dempsey, Lt.-Gen. Sir
Miles, 99, 120, 126, 138,
150
Dives, River, 75 (map), 76,
82, 144, 154, 166
Douve, River, 76
Douvres, 124, 125
Dummies, 56–7, **56–7**
Dummy Invasions, 80–1

E

Eisenhower, Gen, Dwight
D., 10, **10**, 12, **12**, 43, **47**,
66, 68, 150, 154, 175, 180
Elboeuf, 174
Encirclement, 170–5
Epsom *See* Operation
Epsom
Esquay, 152
Eterville, 152
Evrecy, 152

F

Falaise, 49, 51–2, 151,
166
Falaise Pocket, Closure
of, 170–2, 171 (map),
170, **172**, **173**
Fervanches, 162
Feuchtinger, Maj.-Gen.,
110, 120
Fougeres, 149
French Division
2 Armoured, 68, 174
French Resistance, 60,
129, 132

G

Gale, Maj.-Gen., 74
Gassicourt, 167
German Air Force, 19, **39**,
115, 142, 164, 180
German Army
Armies
7: 53, 55, 78, 82, 95,
112, 142, 148, 149,
153, 164, 166, 167,
168
15: 48, 49, 78, 82, 153
167
Corps
47 Panzer: 120
84: 62, 95, 120

Divisions
Panzer Lehr: 35,
48–9, 82, 112, 124,
126, 132, 138, 143,
152, 158, 162, 164
1 SS Panzer: 139, 142,
143, 150, 152, 154,
158, 162, 164, 168
2 SS Panzer: 138, 139,
142, 143, 149, 150,
152, 158, 164, 168
2 Panzer: 124, 131,
132, 140, 152, 164, 168
3 Parachute: 127, 132,
140
5 Parachute: 158
6 Parachute: 167, 174
9 SS Panzer: 142, 143,
144, 150, 152, 162, 164
10 SS Panzer: 139,
142, 143, 144, 150,
152, 164, 168
12 SS Panzer: 48–9,
82, 112, 124, 126,
131, 132, 138, 139,
143, 150, 152, 154,
162, 164, 174
16 GAF: 150
17 GAF: 174
17 SS Panzer-
Grenadier: 124,
130, 132, 137, 164
21 Panzer: **34**, 35,
48–9, 82, 105, 108,
109, 110, 112, 120,
131, 132, 138, 139,
143, 152, 154, 158,
162, 164
77: 127, 132
84 Infantry: 166, 169
85 Infantry: 174
89 Infantry: 166
116 Panzer: 152, 164,
166
243 Infantry: 164
271: 153153, 164
272 Infantry: 153,
158, 164
276: 150, 158
277: 164
326: 158
331 Infantry: 174
344 Infantry: 174
346: 131, 164, 174
348 Infantry: 174
352: 90, 94, 95, 102,
119, 125, 140
353 Infantry: 132,
158, 164
363 Infantry: 166, 169
709: 82
711 Infantry: 174
716: 82, 90, 109, 138
see also Panzers
German Forces in France,
28–38, 29 (map), 48
Facing Allied Front,
June & July: 178
Facing Allied Front,
15 July: 155
Review of Performance,
182–3

German HQs, Siting, 134
German High Command,
168
Conflict in, 32–6
Giraud, Gen., **10**
Glider Pilots, US, **77**
Gliders, **68**, **75**, **79**, **113**
Gold, 43 (map), 67, 69, 86,
100–5, 100 (map), **100–1**,
103–4, 140
Beach Clearance, 102,
104
Museums and Monu-
ments, 186
Naval Bombardment,
100–1
Weather and Tides, 101
Goodwood *See* Operation
Goodwood
Gooseberry Break-
waters, 15–6, 69, 140,
143, 181–2
Grand Hameau, 94
Granville, 162
Graves, 184–7, 184–5
(maps), **187**
Gun Emplacements, **22**,
28, **30**, **31**, **91**, **99**, **103**

H

Hall, Rear-Adm., USN,
90, 93
Harbours, 14–7, **14**, **15**, **17**,
52, 104, 140, **140–1**, 142,
143, 181–2
Harris, Sir Arthur, 150
Haye-du-Puits, 130, 149
Henderbonville, 174
Hermanville sur Mer,
108, 109, **109**
Hitler, Adolf, 32–6, 49,
56, 57, 112, 127, 142, 144,
153, 167, 168, 179, 182
Hobart's 'Funnies', **96–7**
Human Factor, 64–5
Hussars, **101**, **107**, **109**

I

Intelligence, 18, 32, 34,
36
Deception Plan, 33, 36,
56–7, **56–7**, 60–2, 114,
167
Interdiction Programme,
58–60, 60 (map), 114,
180
Inter-Services Co-
operation, Review of,
180–2
Isigny, 125

J

Jeeps, **159**
Juno, 43 (map), 67, 69, 86,
106–8, 119, 126, 140
Monuments, 186

K

Kaltenbrunner, Gen., 36
Krancke,Adm., 57, 58, 80, **81**

L

la Riviere, 102–3, 108
Landing Areas *See*
Assault Areas
Landing Craft, 69, **88–9**,
90, **93**
le Hamel, 102
Le Havre, 174
Le Mans, 149, 166, 170
le Mesnil-Patry, 138
Leigh-Mallory, Air
Marshal Sir Trafford,
12, **12**, 42, 43, 66, 68, **68**
Lessay, 152, 158
Lion-sur-Mer, 108
Lisieux, 166, 174
Loire, 166
Luftwaffe, 19, **39**, 115, 142,
164, 180

M

Maltot, 152
'Man who never was', 36
Manoeuvres, **44–5**, 62, 93
Mantes-Gassicourt, 166,
174, 179
Maquis, 60, **129**, 132
Marshall, Gen. George,
16–7
Master Plan *See under*
Montgomery
Maupertus, 138
Mayenne, 149
Medical Services, 11
see also Casualties
Memorials, 184–7, 184–5
(maps) **187**
Merderet, R., 77, 78, 125
Merchant Navy, Review
of Achievements, 181
Merville, 75 (map), 76
Montebourg, 125, 130, 137
Montgomery, Gen. Sir
Bernard, 12, **12**, **47**,
64–5, **65**, 66, 68, 120,
124, **129**, **134**, 139, 143,
148, **148**, 149, 150, 151,
152, 153, 154, 162, 166,
167, 170, 174
Hands over to Eisen-
hower, 175, 180
HQ, 128, 134–5
Master Plan, 42–55, 46
(map), 50–1 (maps),
55 (map), 132, 144,
145, 178, 179
Controversial
Aspects of, 44,
51–5, 68, 154, 156–7
Main Points of,
Apr. 1944: 50
Philosophy, 53

Monuments, 186
Morgan, Lt.-Gen. F. E., 10
  Criticism of Mont-
    gomery, 54
Mortain, 149, 166
  Counter-attack, 168–9,
    169 (map), 174
Mulberry Harbours, 14–7,
  14, **15**, **17**, 104, 140,
  140–1, 142, **143**, 181–2
Museums, 186

N

Nantes, 164
Naval Bombardments,
  93–4, 100–1, 116–8,
  180–1
  Operations, 62–4, 84,
    116–8
  Command Structure,
    63
  Vessels *See* Landing
    Craft; Ships
Neptune *See* Operation
  Neptune
Netherlands Brigade, 69
Normandy
  Choice of Assault
    Area, 23–4
  Orders for Develop-
    ment of Campaign,
    148
  Pre-Assessment of
    Resistance, 37–8
  Reinforcements, 6 May,
    35
  Review of the Battle,
    178–83
    Eisenhower's
      Opportunity, 183
    Most Important
      Result, 179
  see also specific headings
    e.g. D-Day, Omaha
  'Normandy to the Baltic',
    54
Norway, Deception Plan,
  56
Noyers, 138, 162

O

Odon Bridgehead, 138–40,
  139 (map)
Odon, River, 126, 132,
  151, 152
OKW, 33, 34, 82, 120
Omaha, 42 (map), 45, 46,
  66, 69, 77, 84, 90–6,
  90–5, 119, 125–6, 140
  Casualties, 95, 118, **118**
  Monuments, 186
  Naval Assistance, 93–4,
    181
  Obstacles, 90
  Reasons for Difficul-
    ties, 90, 93, 96
  Terrain, 90–1
  Weather and Tides, 91

Operation
  Bodyguard *See* Decep-
    tion Plan
  Cobra, 148–75
  Epsom, 138–40, 139
    (map)
  Goodwood, 154–7, 155
    (map), 158
  Neptune, 62–4, 84
  Overlord *See* Overlord
Order of Battle, *See* D-Day
Orleans, 174
Orne, River, 43, 74, 75
  (map), 82, 105, 108, 109,
  110, 120, 126, 131, 143,
  150, 151, 152, 153, 166
Ouistreham, 108
Overlord
  Choice of Assault
    areas, 20–5, 21 (map)
  Date, 17, 44, 62–4
  Planning, 40–71; maps:
    42–3, 46, 50–1
  Pre-Assessment of
    Resistance, 37–8
  Preparatory Opera-
    tions, 58–65, 63 (map)
  Prerequisites, 18–9
  see also D-Day Assault

P

Panzers, 48–9, 51, 120,
  121, 136, 139, 142, 143,
  144, 150, 152, 153, 162,
  179
Paratroops, **68**, **76**
Paris, 151, 166, 164
Patton, Lt.-Gen. George,
  55, 57, 68, 164, **165**, **167**,
  170, 179
Pearl Harbor, 11
Périers-sur-le-Dan, 108,
  109, 110, 112, 149, 158
'Phase-line' Controversy,
  53–4, 55 (map)
Plocher, **168**
Pluto, 16
Point du Hoe, 95
Polish 1 Armoured
  Division, 68, 166, 170,
  172
Port-en-Bessin, 43, 119,
  125
Ports *See* Harbours
Pouppeville, 86
Preparatory Operations,
  58–65
Prisoners, **137**, 142, **179**

Q

Quinéville, 43, 130

R

Radar, German, 80–1, **80**
  Jamming, 80–1
Radio Deception, 56–7

Railways, 48, 49, 58–60,
  60
Ramsay, Adm. Sir
  Bertram, 12, **12**, 42,
  43–4, **66**
Rauray, 138, 139, 150
Resistance Movement,
  60, **129**, 132
Rhine, 180
Ridgway, Maj.-Gen. Matt,
  78
Rommel, F.M. Erwin, 28,
  30, **31**, 32, **33**, 34, 112,
  127, 130, **135**, 143, 149,
  153, **168**
Roosevelt, Theodore D.,
  10, **10**
Rouen, 151, 166
RAF Formations
  83 Group, 135, 142
Royal Warwickshires,
  112
Ruhr, 179
Rundstedt *See* von
  Rundstedt

S

St Eny, 258
St Gilles, 162
Ste Honorine la Chard-
  ronnerette, 131, 139
St Laurent, 94, 140, 142,
  181–2
St-Lô, 130, 132, 149, 152,
  158, **159**
Ste Mere Eglise, 77, 78,
  88, 125, 130
St Sauveur, 130
Schweppenburg *See* von
  Schweppenburg
Sée, 168
Seine, Baie de la, 22, 28,
  34, 80
Seine, River, 166, 170,
  175, 175 (map)
Sélune, 168
Seulles, River, 106, 152
SHAEF
  Command Structure,
    13
  Commanders, 12, **12**
Ships
  HMS Ajax, 101
  HMS Faulknor, 128
  HMS Goodson, 142
  HMS Nelson, 181
  HMS Ramillies, 181
  USS Augusta, **89**
Shropshire Light Infan-
  try, 112
Smuts, F.M. Jan, 66, **128**
Somme Estuary, 22
Special Air Service
  (SAS), 132, 151
Speidel, Lt.-Gen. Hans,
  33, 78, 82, **168**
Sperrle, **168**
Spitfire, 20, **20**
Staffordshire Yeomanry,
  112

Statistics
  D-Day, 115–6
  6–12 June, 127
  15–22 June, 140
  6–30 June, 142
  D-Day – 31 Aug, 182
  Merchant Navy, 181
  See also Casualties,
    Losses
Submarines, 62, 64
  Midget, 64
Sword, 43 (map), 67, 69,
  74, 82, 86, 108–12, 119,
  120, 126, 140
  Monuments and
    Museums, 186

T

Tanks, 91–3, 96, **96**–7,
  101–3, **103**–4, **107**, 110,
  111, **170**
  see also Panzers
Task Forces
  Eastern, 66–7, 82, 84,
    98–112
  Western, 66, 84, 86–96,
    93, **116**–7
Taylor, Maj.-Gen. Max-
  well, 78
Taute, River, 152
Tedder, A.C.M. Sir
  Arthur, **12**, **47**, 52, **52**, 135
  Criticisms by, 54, 144, 145
Teller mine, **30**
Tessel, 139
Tides, 84, 86, 91, 101–2,
  106, 140
Tilley-sur-Seulles, 126,
  131, 138, 150
Tourville-sur-Odon, 138
Training, 44–5, 62, 93
Transport, German prob-
  lems, 48, **48**–9
Troarn, 154

U

U Boats, 62, 142
Ultra, 18, 32, 34
Underground Movements
  60, **129**, 132
Underwater Obstacles,
  23, 28–31, 86, 90, 98, **107**,
  116
US Air Force
  8: 83, 144, 154
  9: **79**, 83, 142, 154
US Army
  12 Army Group, 166
  21 Army Group, 174
  Armies
    1: 42–3, 42 (map), 46,
      49, 51–2, 66, 68,
      119, 124, 128, 132,
      136, 140, 142, 143,
      148, 149, 152, 158,
      158 (map), 162,
      163 (map), 166,
      168, 174

3: 49, 68, 162, 164, 166, 168, 170, 174
Corps
  5: 47, 90, 124, 125–6, 130, 131, 143, 151, 162, 174
  7: 47, 77, 78, 86, **87**, 88, 124–5, 130, 138, 149, 152, 162
  8 130, 149, 152, 162
  15: 132, 149, 152, 162
  15: 132, 170, 174
  19: 130, 152, 174
Divisions
  1: 91, 92, 95, 125, 126
  2: 126, 130
  4: 86–8, 125, 130, 137
  9: **87**, 124, 125–6 130, 137
  29: 91, 95, 125, 126, 130
  30: 130, 163
  79: 137, 149
  82 Airborne: 68, 74, 76–8, **76**–7, 82–3, 88, 124, 125, 130
  90: 130
  101 Airborne: 68, 74, 76–8, **76**–7, 82–3, 86, 88, 124, 125, 126, 130
Rangers, 91, 95, 96
Utah, 42 (map), 44, 66, 68, 69, 78, 83, 84, 86–8, **87**–9, 98, 119, **119**, 124–5, **179**
Museums and Monuments, 186

V

V-bomb, threat, 35
V1, **35**, 179
Valognes, 137
Vannes, 164
Varreville, 88
Vaucelles, 150
Vernon, 174
Vian, R.-Adm. Sir Philip, 99
Vierville, 94,
Villers-Bocage, 126, 131
Vimont, 154
Vire, 162, 166
Vire, River, 43, 124, 125, 143, 149, 152
von Kluge, F.M., **168**, 169
von Rundstedt, F.M.
  Carl, 28, 31–5, **33**, **34**, 78, 82, 112, 117, **135**, **143**, 144, 169
von Schweppenburg, 32, 33, **168**

W

Weather, 64, 84, 132, 139, 140, 140–1, 141–2, 155, 169
'Window', 81
Wireless Deception, 56–7

GLOSSARY

The definitions given here are those that would have accurately described the use of the terms during the latter part of the Second World War.

Army	A military formation comprising two or more CORPS.
Army Group	A military formation comprising two or more ARMIES.
Assault Unit . . .	of Royal Engineers. A unit of tracked armoured vehicles with special equipment designed for dealing with beach, and other, defences.
Battalion (Bn)	Consists of three or four companies of infantry.
Brigade (Bde)	Consists of three or four battalions of infantry. Also, three regiments of armoured troops.
Corps	A military formation usually comprising two or more DIVISIONS.
Division (Div)	Three brigades of infantry or two brigades of armoured and mobile infantry troops.
Enfilade	Referring to the flanks of a military unit or formation: hence, enfilade fire – fire brought to bear on the flanks of troops or troop emplacements.
Fascine	A large bundle of timber and metal rods carried on the front of a tank. The fascine can be dropped into a hole to enable vehicles to cross over.
Flail Tank	A tank equipped with a front-mounted rotary chain flail designed to explode land mines in the tanks path.
Hull-Down	A position adopted by a tank commander in which the body of his vehicle is hidden from view with only the turret and gun visible from the front.
Interdiction	The undertaking of measures designed to obstruct and delay the movement of enemy troops and supplies, by air-bombing, sabotage and long-range shelling.
OKW	Oberkommando der Wehrmacht. Hitler's own personal military HQ.
Panzer (Division)	German armoured division.
Panzer Lehr (Division)	Lehr, in German, means 'training' but in fact this division was one of the most powerful of its kind in the German Army. On D-Day, it had 190 tanks, 45 assault guns and more than 600 armoured half-tracks.
Regiment (other than infantry)	Normally consists of three batteries of artillery or or three squadrons of tanks.
Regimental Combat Team (RCT)	An American fighting unit of roughly the same strength as a British BRIGADE of three (sometimes four) battalions. The RCT includes certain supporting weapons which in the case of a British brigade would be allocated from separate specialist units.
Schwerpunkt	German. The centre-line or focus of an attack; the principal thrust line.
Staff Organisation	In the British Army, the three Staff Branches are: 'G' = General Staff, concerned with operations, planning, staff duties and intelligence; 'A' = Adjutant-General's Staff, dealing with all personnel matters and with discipline, and 'Q' = Quarter-Master-General's Staff, responsible for all supplies and for transportation other than unit transport. The Services include Medical, Ordnance, Electrical and Mechanical, Transport and Catering.
Unit	A BATTALION of infantry, or a REGIMENT of armoured troops, or of artillery. An independent Company, particularly of Engineers, Signals or Transport.

Acknowledgements

ARTISTS: Harry Clow, Tony Graham
RETOUCHER: Roy Flooks

Photographs are credited page by page and, where appropriate, left to right or by descending order of baseline. Principal sources of illustration are indicated by the following abbreviations: Imperial War Museum, London (IWM); United States Army Archives (USAA); United States Navy Archives (USN); United States Air Force (USAF); Public Archives of Canada (PAC); John McClancy Press (JMP); Robert Hunt Library (RHL); Bundesarchiv, Koblenz (BAK); Ullstein Bilderdienst, Berlin (UBB).

Chapter title pages:

8 IWM British troops reading a booklet on France issued just before embarkation, 7 June '44.

26 JMP. Heavily protected German guns dominating the approach to the French coast.

40 IWM. General Montgomery with his senior commanders, including Dempsey and Crerar, photographed 22 June '44.

72 IWM. Hand-picked 'Pathfinder' pilots synchronise watches before take-off; June '44. From left Lieutenants Bobby de Latour, Don Wells, John Vischer and Bob Midwood.

122 IWM. Cromwell and Sherman tanks, and three-ton lorries, head inland from Arromanches.

146 USAA. British and American troops meet up at Chambois, 19 Aug '44. Lt. Harold Ashby, in command of a British armoured unit, with Maj. Harold Delp and Lt.-Col. Carl Diely, both of US Army 5 Corps.

176 RHL. Freedom comes to Bayeux. 7 July '44. Citizens of liberated Bayeux read a copy of the free newspaper *La Renaissance du Bayeux*.

10 IWM, USAA. **11** USN. **12** RHL/London News Agency. **15** IWM. **17** IWM. **18** IWM. **19** USAF. **20** RHL. **22** RHL. **23** RHL. **24** BAK. **25** USAA, PAC. **28** UBB. **29** UBB. **30** BAK, USAA. **31** UBB, UBB, UBB. **33** UBB, BAK. **34** BAK, BAK. **35** JMP. **36** UBB. **37** RHL. **38** JMP. **39** JMP, JMP. **44** USAA. **45** USN. **47** United Press International. **48** RHL. **49** BAK. **52** UPI. **56–57** RHL, RHL, RHL. **58** IWM. **59** IWM. **60** USAA. **61** USAF. **65** USN. **68** IWM. **68–69** IWM. **69** USAA. **75** IWM. **76** USAA. **77** USN. **79** USAF. **80** UBB. **81** UBB. **83** USAF. **87** USN. **88–89** USN. **89** USAA. **90** USN, JMP. **91** USAA. **92** USN. **93** USAA. **94** IWM. **95** USAA. **96** IWM. **97** IWM. **99** UBB. **101** IWM. **103** IWM, USN. **104** IWM. **107** IWM. **109** IWM. **111** BAK, Keystone Press. **113** IWM, IWM. **117** US Coast Guard. **118** USN. **119** USAA. **121** RHL. **125** USAA. **128** USAA. **129** IWM. **131** IWM. **133** Keystone Press. **134** IWM. **135** BAK. **137** USAA. **141** USAA, USAA. **143** IWM. **148** IWM. **150–51** IWM. **157** IWM. **159** JMP, IWM. **164** IWM. **165** JMP. **167** RHL. **168** BAK, BAK. **170** PAC. **172** BAK. **173** PAC. **175** USAA. **179** USAA. **186** Commonwealth War Graves Commission.

BIBLIOGRAPHY

BERNARD, Professor Henri. *Guerre Totale at Guerre Révolutionnaire*; Brepols, Belgium, 1966.

BRADLEY, General Omar. *A Soldier's Story*; Holt, New York, 1951.

BRERETON, Lieut.-Gen. Lewis H. *The Brereton Diaries*; Morrow, New York, 1946.

Chronology of the Second World War; Royal Institute of International Affairs, London, 1947.

CHURCHILL, Winston S. *The Second World War*; Cassel, London, 1948–51.

EISENHOWER, General Dwight D. *Crusade in Europe*; Doubleday, New York, 1948

FARAGO, Ladislas. *Patton*; Dell, New York, 1965.

GUINGAND, Maj.-Gen. Sir Francis de. *Operation Victory*; Hodder & Stoughton, London, 1947. *Generals at War*; Hodder & Stoughton, London, 1964.

History of the Second World War; Official Military History Series, HMSO, London, 1954–62.

KINGSTON–McCLOUGHRY, Air Marshall E. J. *The Direction of War*; Jonathan Cape, London, 1954.

LIDELL HART, Captain B. H. *The Other Side of the Hill*; Cassell, London 1951.

MONTGOMERY, Field–Marshal Viscount. *Memoirs*; Collins, London, 1958. *El Alamein to the Sangro*; and *Normandy to the Baltic*; Military Editions, Bielefeld, BRD, 1946.

NORTH, John. *N.W. Europe 1944–5*; HMSO, London, 1953.

RAMSAY, Admiral Sir Bertram. *The Assault Phase of the Normandy Landings*; London Gazette, 1948.

ROSKILL, Stephen. *Churchill and the Admirals*; Collins, London, 1977.

RYAN, Cornelius. *The Longest Day*; Gollancz, London 1960. *A Bridge Too Far*; Hamish Hamilton, London, 1974.

SPEIDEL, Hans. *We Defended Normandy*; Jenkins, 1951.

TUTE, Warren. *D Day*; Sidgewick & Jackson, London.

WILMOT, Chester. *The Struggle for Europe*; Collins, London, 1965.